I0949980

THE FUTURE OF RELIGION
IN AMERICA

# GOD

# IS

# ALIVE

# AND WELL

## FRANK NEWPORT

GALLUP PRESS

1251 Avenue of the Americas

23rd Floor

New York, NY 10020

Library of Congress Control Number: 2012945501

ISBN: 978-1-59562-062-0  5038 2331 12/12

First Printing: 2012

10 9 8 7 6 5 4 3 2 1

*This book is dedicated to George H. Gallup Jr. (1930-2011)*

# Table of Contents

Introduction: Religion Is the Elephant in the Room....................1

Chapter I: In God We Still Trust...............................9

Chapter II: America Remains a Christian Nation,
        But Different Now..............................21

Chapter III: Religion Is Good for Your Health.........................47

Chapter IV: Religion and Politics..............................73

Chapter V: Age and Religion: The Fascinating Relationship ..103

Chapter VI: State Cultures of Religion: Why Mississippi Is
        Vastly Different From Vermont .........................143

Chapter VII: Men and Women...............................169

Chapter VIII: Religion Is a Class Act ......................203

Chapter IX: The Potential for a More Direct Influence
        of Religion .................................229

Chapter X: Summing it Up: The Future of Religion ...............241

References .........................................251

Acknowledgements ...............................275

About the Author .................................279

# INTRODUCTION

## Religion Is the Elephant in the Room

Religion is a fundamental part of our American society. But, like most aspects of society, it is changing. This book is my attempt to look ahead and understand what those changes are.

Most Americans have some semblance of religiousness. Most believe in God, and the vast majority attends some type of religious services in an average year. This underlying religiousness sits there as potential, albeit dormant, energy for many Americans. For many others, religion is converted into kinetic, activated energy manifested in all aspects of their lives. I believe this activated religiousness could become more and more common in the years ahead. America is likely to become a more religious nation, but one in which religion is practiced in different ways. And religion may well have an increasingly important impact on American life.

Unlike citizens of most other countries in the world, Americans group themselves into hundreds of distinct micro religious groups and denominations. These groups are constantly evolving, splitting like amoeba to form new groups related to social status, geography, politics, and social and political attitudes. The most common pattern today is the development of the "no name" religious group: Americans who worship only under the banner of their nondenominational predilections. This comes at the cost of traditional religious groups, including most prominently, mainline Protestant denominations. Additionally, more Americans today simply claim to have no formal religious identity at all.

Change is coming as the massive baby boom generation ages into its 60s and 70s — auguring for a religious boom or bust depending on the religious path this group takes as it reaches senior status. I think baby boomers will choose the religious path — by sheer numbers alone shifting the country into a more religious mode.

At the same time, the demographics of the younger generation are changing as well. Fewer younger Americans are marrying, and the birth rate has been declining — and both of these factors are related to religiousness. The growing population of young, religious Hispanic Americans could also substantially affect religiousness in the U.S.

Change may also be coming as Americans recognize that religion promotes exactly what medical experts are calling for to address the nation's healthcare problems — healthier eating, less worry and stress, exercise, higher wellbeing, and better physical health. Religious Americans have better physical and emotional wellbeing than others and are less likely to be depressed.

Americans are also migrating to more religious states of the union and in many instances, adopting their new states' religious norms.

Religion has evolved into a potent political force for conservatives and Republicans. I think it's likely that liberals and Democrats will wake up to these facts and begin an epic battle for religious Americans' political allegiance.

Specific and definable subgroups of the American population are reliably more religious than others. Women are more religious than men, potentially escalating tensions in religions that often exclude women from positions of leadership — mainly Catholics and fundamentalist Protestant groups. Upscale Americans are less personally religious than those who are less well-off but equally as likely to go to church, thus taking advantage of the community aspects of religion. This pattern is likely to expand in the years ahead.

The ethnic composition of America is changing. Blacks, the most religious segment of American society, may not experience rapid growth, but Hispanics, also more religious than average, demonstrably will.

My goal in this book is to figure out what these patterns can tell us about the causes and functions of religion and its future. The foundation for the book is the perspective of science — using empirical data to analyze what people think and do about religion. *God Is Alive and Well* is based in large part on hundreds of thousands of interviews Gallup has conducted in recent years — interviews that asked Americans about their religion, their religious beliefs, and their religious behavior. The resulting data provide an unparalleled and unprecedented database of information about Americans and their religions.

Not everyone thinks these types of data are valuable. Critics of religion such as Richard Dawkins, the late Christopher Hitchens, Sam Harris, and others claim, in essence, that it doesn't really matter what people say about religion because what they say is not reality. People may think they are religious, that there is a God, and that their religious rituals make perfect sense. But what people don't know, according to these neo-atheist thinkers, is that they have been duped. This view basically assumes that humans don't know what they are talking about. Atheists like Dawkins maintain that humans' religious consciousness has been hijacked by biology and evolution — parts of our inherited brains. These parts, developed through evolution and passed down to us through our genes, capture our overt consciousness and make it more receptive to the false idea of God and religion.

Thus, the atheists would argue, when the passengers on US Airways Flight 1549, famously piloted by Capt. Chesley "Sully" Sullenberger, began to pray as their plane descended into the Hudson River or when — as I will discuss in this book — most Americans tell us that they believe in God, that they pray, and that they attend church, they are only reflecting inner delusions.

The issue is not that people have religious beliefs and engage in religious behaviors. Dawkins et. al. recognize those facts of life. The issue is causality. Dawkins and others say that religious consciousness is a false consciousness brought about by evolution and superstition. It is no accident that the title of a Dawkins bestselling book is *The God Delusion*. Those who are religious, of course, say that religious consciousness results from a divine force, God.

I will not be able to prove the existence of God, but I will show that many, many Americans believe that God exists and act and think accordingly. If people believe in God and the spiritual realm and heaven and hell, then the consequences in their daily lives are quite real, regardless of their ultimate reality. As social psychologist W.I. Thomas said: "If men define situations as real, they are real in their consequences."

I will not be able to fully answer the question of what is behind Americans' religious consciousness. No one — to my knowledge — has measured God with a scientific instrument. Nobody has seen God in a way that can be verified independently. There is little evidence to document that heaven and hell exist. And we still don't know how many angels can dance on the head of a pin.

But should millions of Americans' statements of religious belief and behavior be dismissed with a flick of the pen? I don't think so. The pattern of religious influence in American society to me suggests mass consequences rather than mass delusion. In this book, I will examine those consequences.

## WHY THIS BOOK FOR THIS AUTHOR?

A young Frank Newport was fascinated many years ago when I first read anthropologist Horace Miner's famous article "Body Ritual Among the Nacirema." In his piece, Miner described — in great detail — the strange customs and rituals of a peculiar tribe called the Nacirema "living in the territory between the Canadian Cree, the Yaqui and Tarahumare of Mexico, and the Carib and Arawak of the Antilles."

After lovingly analyzing the strange behaviors and odd rituals of this tribe, Miner hits the reader with his punch line: The weird tribe he was describing was none other than the tribe American (Nacirema spelled backward).

The article grabbed my attention because it highlighted one of the most appealing aspects of social science — the ability to take a new look at the society around us from an outside, objective perspective. As Robert Burns said, "Oh, would some Power the gift give us/to see ourselves as others see us!" We humans tend to view the world we construct and live in as normal, standard, and unexceptional; we take it for granted. Viewed from afar, however, our world can seem quite curious indeed. Miner's clever piece tapped into my underlying fascination with the abstract study of our own culture.

I couple that fascination with a quite intense personal background in religion. Religion was a major part of my life from the dawn of my consciousness. My father was a Southern Baptist minister and professional theologian who spent his entire adult life studying and theorizing about religion. I have a whole host of religious predecessors on my mother's side of the family as well. I was brought up religious, went to church about three times a week minimum, attended Baylor University — the world's largest Baptist university — and in many ways spent my formative years steeped in a religious approach to life.

I could, in fact, have become a professionally religious person myself — attended a seminary or a divinity school, became a minister, or taught religion in a theological institution.

But I didn't. Instead, I rather quickly drifted into a more objective, neutral study of the phenomenon of religion. I moved into the field of sociology, the scientific analysis of human social behavior. I studied and taught the sociology of religion, published books and articles in the field, and have continued to focus on the scientific study of humans and their religion ever since.

Why? Because I am convinced that religion is incredibly important. Religious beliefs and rituals are a highly embedded and powerful component of American culture and social structure, one that I think is likely to become even more so in the years ahead.

Studying religion using the tools of science is not always easy. Data about religion are not always easy to come by.

There is little official data from the U.S. Census Bureau, which is constitutionally prohibited from asking questions about religion.

As the Census Bureau states: "Public Law 94-521 prohibits us from asking a question on religious affiliation on a mandatory basis; therefore, the Bureau of the Census is not the source for information on religion."

But there is also good news: Scientists have taken matters into their own hands by measuring what people tell us about religion in their personal lives. There is an enormous corpus of nongovernmental scientific survey data on what we can call the observables of religion.

One of these scientists was Dr. George Gallup, the founder of The Gallup Poll, who early on included questions about religion in his surveys of Americans. His son, George Gallup Jr., spent a good deal of his life immersed in polling data and what they tell us about Americans' religion. Some of the resulting Gallup data go back to the 1940s. Since 2008, we have the unique advantage of a massive Gallup Daily tracking project involving 1,000 interviews a night, more than 350,000 interviews a year — interviews that include questions about Americans' religion. I will use the aggregation of these interviews as the basis for this book.

To examine religion in America, I am using a very specific research tool and approach — the scientific analysis of the expressed religiousness of randomly selected samples of hundreds of thousands of Americans. There are other ways to look at religion, but the ability of our samples to project to all Americans gives us the unique capability to study religion based on the attitudes and behaviors of the entire population.

I hope you will agree with me that it is a fascinating journey, one that will help us all better understand one of the most potent and important forces in our American society.

# CHAPTER I

## In God We Still Trust

### AMERICA TODAY IS STILL A LARGELY RELIGIOUS NATION

Many years ago, in the months after the June 1944 D-Day invasion of France and just before the Battle of the Bulge in Europe, Dr. George Gallup decided to ask Americans back on the home front a simple five-word question: "Do you believe in God?" Dr. Gallup liked his questions short and to the point. This simple question, at a very basic level, picked up on the fundamentals of religious potential in this country. Gallup's 1944 survey showed that 96% of Americans responded "yes," they did believe in God. Only 1% said "no," with a few respondents hesitating or saying that they had no opinion — a ringing affirmation of the belief in God.

Fast forward to 2011 — a very different world that has gone through decades of change. Although wars are still being fought, there is nothing like the conflagration that was World War II. The world is much more sophisticated, technologically advanced, skeptical. *Time* magazine published a cover story titled "Is God Dead?" in the 1960s. Books are published with names like *God Is Not Great: How Religion Poisons Everything*, and, as noted earlier,

*The God Delusion.* Certainly, the percentage of Americans who believe in God would be lower now, right?

Not by much. More than nine in 10 Americans still said "yes" when asked the basic question "Do you believe in God?" in May 2011. This is down only slightly from the 1940s, when Gallup first asked this question.

Despite the many changes that have rippled through American society over the past several decades, belief in God, at least as measured in this direct way, has remained high and relatively stable.

In 1976, Gallup used a slightly different question, asking: "Do you believe in God or a universal spirit?" Back then, 94% of Americans agreed. That percentage stayed fairly steady through 1994. In the May 2011 survey, 91% of Americans agreed, and 8% said "no."

As you have figured out by this point, the percentage of Americans who definitively say there is no God is generally 6% to 8%, no matter how we ask the question. Defiant atheism among ordinary Americans is minimal — despite a few doubts about exactly what form God may take.

Now let me share some other indications that religion continues to matter and remains an important part of American society. One of these indicators is attendance at religious services. Gallup has in one way or another asked Americans about their church attendance since the 1930s, way back to the Great Depression.

Church attendance peaked in the 1950s, when self-reported church attendance was higher than it had been before and higher than it has been since. But self-reported church attendance today is actually not much lower than it has been at most other points in time, including during the Great Depression. In fact, a 1940 Gallup survey showed that about the same percentage of Americans reported attending religious services then as is the case today.

About 40% of Americans — sometimes a little more, sometimes a little less — say they attend religious services at least once a week or almost weekly. About 15% of Americans say that they never attend church. Overall, this is fairly indicative of a religious nation.

Gallup has asked Americans since the 1950s if they believe that religion can answer all or most of today's problems or if they believe that religion is largely old-fashioned and out of date. In the 1950s and 1960s, more people said that religion can answer all or most of the day's problems than say that today. But over the last 25 years, there hasn't been a lot of change. About six in 10 Americans consistently say that religion can answer life's problems.

The number of Americans who say religion is very important in their daily lives dropped substantially between 1952, when Gallup first asked this question, and the late 1970s. From that point on, there have been some ups and downs, but they have not been dramatic. Importance of religion actually increased slightly at points over the last several decades from its low point in the late 1970s. More recently, it has nudged down. But at 55% today, it's no lower than it was 30 years ago. There is no indication that there has been a continuous drop in the personal aspect of religion in recent years.

When we put it all together, we get the image of a basically religious American population whose underlying religiousness has not changed a lot in recent decades. There seems to have been a religious upswing of sorts in the 1950s and into the early 1960s but a general period of stability in the decades since.

## THE RISE OF THE "NONES"

There are, of course, exceptions to every rule. Studying human behavior, as I do, is often humbling. I am humbled here to point out that we do have one measure of religion that *has* shown change over time: the percentage of Americans who are variously called "unaffiliated," "nones," or the "non-identifiers." This is "The Rise of the Nones," which sounds like a bad movie title.

Imagine that your phone rings and it is a Gallup interviewer. During the interview, which of course you graciously consent to do, the interviewer asks you: "What is your religious preference — are you Protestant, Roman Catholic, Mormon, Jewish, Muslim, another religion, or no religion?"

If you say "another religion," you would be asked: "Would that fall under the general category of Protestant religions, is it a Christian religion, but not Protestant, or is it something else?" Gallup often goes beyond that point and asks non-Catholic Christians to name their denomination.

Between 13% and 14% of Americans say they have no religious identity, and another 3% to 4% say they don't know what their preference is. If you go back to the 1950s, by contrast, nearly *everybody* responded to the question with a religious identity. The percentage of Americans who respond "no religion" when asked this question has grown from near zero in the 1950s to 13% to 14% in 2010 and 2011.

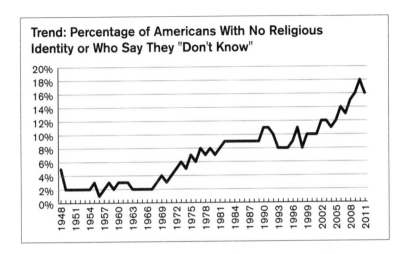

**Trend: Percentage of Americans With No Religious Identity or Who Say They "Don't Know"**

Those who have no religious identity have been heavily scrutinized in recent years. This is partially because social scientists like change, and this change is a highly reliable finding — it can be replicated repeatedly. The rise in "no identity" responders is remarkably constant across survey organizations, which is always a good thing in survey science. Regardless of who does the asking, or how the question is asked, fewer Americans today have a religious "brand" to which they claim allegiance.

What does this mean? You might think the reason for the rise in the nones is pretty straightforward: Americans are simply less religious now than they were in previous decades. But remember, other indicators of religiousness don't follow this same downward trajectory. So we have to pause before making the assumption that the rise in the nones is a clear-cut indicator of a decrease in religiousness.

In fact, a lot of social scientists are uncertain about the meaning of the rise in the nones. Sociologists Chaeyoon Lim, Carol Ann MacGregor, and Robert D. Putnam had this to say recently, "There is little consensus on what the rise of nones means for religion in America."

Let's try to shed some light on this.

Remember that a higher percentage of Americans say they believe in God than say they have a religious identity. This means by definition that there is a gap — some people who believe in God do not have a religious identity. Not all non-identifiers are atheists or anti-religionists. In fact, as many of those who don't have a religious identity in our Gallup surveys say they believe in God as say they don't.

Other researchers find similar patterns, and some go so far as to call the non-identifiers "unchurched believers." Researchers at the Pew Research Center put it this way recently: "The unaffiliated population is a very diverse group. Not all those who are unaffiliated lack spiritual beliefs or religious behaviors; in fact, roughly four-in-ten unaffiliated individuals say religion is at least somewhat important in their lives. … a significant number of those who left their childhood faith and have become unaffiliated leave open the possibility that they may one day join a religion. Among both those who were raised Catholic and Protestant who are now unaffiliated, for example, roughly one-in-three say they just have not found the right religion yet."

All of this points to a simple conclusion: When Americans answer the "what is your religion" question by saying "none," it doesn't *necessarily* mean that they are devoid of religiousness. A "none" response could also mean that the respondents simply don't belong to a formal religious organization, group, or denomination. Or it could mean that they don't choose to label themselves with the name of a formal religious organization, group, or denomination. The "none" in these instances reflects how the respondents wanted to view themselves or how they chose to express their religion, *not* necessarily an absence of religiousness.

Remember what we are dealing with here: a decrease in the percentage of Americans who verbally offer up the specific name of a religious group or denomination when asked what their religion is. In other words, a verbal report of an aspect of themselves. In this case, religion.

What if I asked you to name your ethnic background? That's not something we can easily determine through a blood test. It's not written on your passport. Like most people, you probably have different strains of nationality. It's up to you to choose how you want to see yourself. I have British and French ancestors. When asked, I have to choose which of these, or both, I want to claim as my ancestry. In the same way, you have to choose how you want to portray yourself when asked about your religion.

So, the "rise of the nones" in recent years essentially means that people are changing how they identify their religion when they are asked about it. Why? One of two reasons: First, it could reflect a basic decrease in Americans' religiousness — a rise, as it were, of Richard Dawkins-types in the U.S. population. Second, it could reflect a change in how Americans choose to label their religious identity — and nothing at all about how religious they are underneath it all. In other words, a change in how people *report* on their personal religiousness.

Remember that a number of other indicators have not shown a decrease in religion in recent years. This calls into question the first reason. The rise of the nones has occurred even though — to use one of my examples — there has been no concomitant rise in the number of Americans who say they don't believe in God.

That leaves the second explanation. Americans today may simply feel more comfortable saying they don't have a religious identity than they did in past decades. *The uptick in the number of Americans claiming to have no religious identity may be less of a change in the basic religiousness of the American population compared with 60 years ago and more of a change in Americans' "truth in reporting."* In other words, "no religious identity" was hidden back in the 1950s and 1960s. But today, it has come out in the open.

In the 1950s, there were fairly rigid social norms and pressures to conform. Americans in that time period may have felt compelled to respond to questions about their religious identity with a ready answer, regardless of how infrequently they attended church or how unimportant religion might have been to them. When a Gallup interviewer called you in 1956 or 1965 and asked you what your religion was, you were not about to say "none." You said "Catholic" or "Baptist" because that is how you were raised — even if you had not been to church since you were a baby. Today when a Gallup interviewer calls you, you feel much freer to say "none." Americans today — it appears — find it much easier to say what they think.

There are other examples of this difference in a reported number measuring something and the reality of that something underneath it all. Crime rates, for example, are usually based on *reported* crimes. It is possible that a crime rate could go up in a city because more effort is put into finding criminals, not because there has been a change in the underlying actual *incidence* of crime. If the police department in a given city floods the streets with officers who are told that they must arrest people for jaywalking, the crime rate for jaywalking will skyrocket, even if the actual number of people jaywalking stayed the same.

Then there is the case of presidential candidates, who are under some pressure to have a *public* religious identity. I am in fact not aware of any major candidate for president in recent years who has dared say publicly that he or she did not have a religion. No wonder. Gallup surveys show that one of the biggest turnoffs for American voters would be a presidential candidate who explicitly said that he or she was an atheist. Thus, no matter what they may be underneath it all, presidential candidates — when asked — almost always have a specific religious identity.

We noncandidates don't have the same pressures. We are freer to say "none." The increase in "no religious identity" is not meaningless. It reinforces a drift away from organized formal religion into more casual, less formal religion. When it comes to religion, Americans today feel less inclined to want anything to do with a formal or organized religion and more inclined to "wing it." Americans are moving away from "brands" of religion. But all of this does not necessarily mean that Americans are, underneath it all, becoming less religious.

## NO SURVEYS 200 YEARS AGO

America is more than 230 years old. Gallup's 64+-year trend on religious identity represents only a fraction of this history. Sadly, the Founding Fathers were demonstrably deficient when it came to funding public opinion polls. We thus have no scientific survey baseline stretching back over the centuries. There is no systematic way to compare our current data with how Americans in the days of George Washington or Abraham Lincoln would have identified their religion. The number of Americans who had no religious identity in early American history is thus a big unknown.

We do know that there have been significant broad changes in religiousness over the years. We know this because historians keep talking about great revivals and "Great Awakenings," at least three of which have occurred in U.S. history according to those who study such things. To have a revival or an awakening, one must, by definition, be previously "unrevived" or "unawake." The existence of these revivals therefore suggests religious "sleep and wake" cycles. The level of religiosity, or at least outward manifestations of religion in this country, may constantly be in flux — ebbing, flowing, and changing over time.

A couple of social scientists have tried to figure out just how religious Americans were "in the old days." Rodney Stark is a sociologist at Baylor University in Texas, and Roger Finke is a sociologist at Penn State University. Finke was Stark's research assistant at the University of Washington. Before they both changed places of employment, the two men worked together for a number of years trying to develop a systematic understanding of religion and church membership in the United States — going back all the way to 1776.

Because there were no polls conducted in the 1700s and 1800s to speak of, Stark and Finke couldn't trend the types of questions we have today in which we simply ask Americans to name their religion and tell us how often they go to church. They decided instead to rely on estimates of the number of churches that existed in our country's distant past and estimates of the number of members per church. They calculated "adherence rates," or church membership as a percentage of the U.S. population.

Their bottom line, which may surprise some people, was that America was quite *nonreligious* in the olden days. They stated: "What we do find to be the master trend of American religious history is a long, slow, and consistent increase in religious participation from 1776 to 1926 — with the rate inching up slightly after 1926 and then hovering near 60 percent." As Stark has said, "Church membership today is far higher than it was in colonial times, and ... the membership rate has been rising for more than two hundred years."

Church membership is just one measure of religiousness. But it's clear that we can't make the assumption that most Americans had a religious identity 100 or 200 years ago.

---

## Bottom Line

Some people may want to talk about America as a secularizing nation, but just how secular it has become since its founding is not something we can determine precisely. The big change is the increase in the number of Americans who say they have no religious identity. But we don't know where things stand from a larger perspective. We still find that Americans are very religious overall. I like to say that Americans have potential religious energy locked up, ready to be converted to activated energy if and when the time is right. This sets the stage for future religious developments.

# CHAPTER II

## America Remains a Christian Nation, But Different Now

Schools today take great pains to include celebrations of non-Christian holidays along with the traditional December celebration of Christmas. It's becoming more and more common to talk about the holiday season rather than the Christmas season. Sensitive Americans try valiantly to avoid saying "Merry Christmas" and instead say "Happy Holidays."

All of this is the attempt, guided by honorable principles, to give recognition to religious groups that in fact make up very small percentages of the U.S. population. This may surprise you, but America remains a very Christian nation. Nearly 80% of all Americans, according to Gallup data, can be classified within one of two big groups: Catholics and Protestants/other non-Catholic Christians. Given that about 16% of Americans have no religious identity, we can say that 95% of Americans who have a religion are Christians.

Let me repeat these two numbers: 80% of *all Americans* are Christians, and 95% of *all Americans who have a religion* are Christian. The first number has definitely changed over time. More and more Americans, as we have seen, don't have any religious identity at all. This has, for the most part, resulted in fewer Americans who identify as Christians. That 80% — the percentage of all Americans who are Christian — would have been well above 90% 50 years ago.

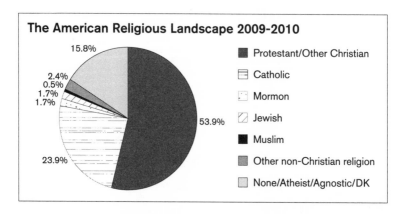

**The American Religious Landscape 2009-2010**

- 53.9% Protestant/Other Christian
- 23.9% Catholic
- 1.7% Mormon
- 1.7% Jewish
- 0.5% Muslim
- 2.4% Other non-Christian religion
- 15.8% None/Atheist/Agnostic/DK

Remarkably, the percentage *of those who have a religion* who are Christian — more than nine in 10 — has *not* changed much over time. The "religious identity pie" is shrinking, to be sure, but its broad composition is not changing. Back in the early 1950s, 90%+ of Americans who had a religion were Christian. Fast forward to today. We find about the same thing.

Suppose you had stopped random people on the street back in the 1950s and asked them their religion. Almost everyone would have told you they had a religion. Furthermore, most of those religions would have been Christian in one way or another. Venture back out into the streets of America today. Once again, stop people randomly. Now nearly one in six people would tell you that they have no religious identity. That marks a big change. But, of those who did have a religion, as was case in the 1950s, most would be Christian.

The percentage of *all* Americans who say they are Christian has declined over time, but that's mainly the result of more and more Americans not having *any* religion. Among Americans with a religion, most were and remain Christian.

It certainly may seem that in recent years we've seen a substantial influx of people into the U.S. who identify with a non-Christian religion — in particular, Muslims and religions associated with Asian countries. But this hasn't had a substantial impact on the religious composition of the country. The number of Americans who maintain an active identity with a non-Christian religion has remained relatively constant — and small — in recent decades.

The percentage of American Jews in the population has contracted from about 4% in 1948 to about 2% today. Muslims are an even smaller proportion of the population, although it's challenging for pollsters to estimate the percentage of American Muslims because some may not speak English, and others are leery of survey inquiries. And those who identify as Hindu, Buddhist, or other non-Christian religions are very small proportions of the population.

All in all, Americans who identify with a non-Christian religion constitute about 5% of all Americans. Again, this is not too far off from where it was decades ago.

It is worth reemphasizing our basic finding: *Most Americans who have a religion are Christian, but the total number of Christians has shrunk because the group of Americans who have no formal religious identity has increased.* Non-Christian religions have not swooped in and become more dominant in the U.S. There has been no apparent wholesale conversion to non-Christian religions. In short, the shrinking of the "Christian pie" is mainly the result of an increase in the "nones" I discussed in the previous chapter.

## CATHOLICS AND PROTESTANTS

America's Christian pie is made up of many different brands of Christianity — too many to list here. Most of these denominations are micro brands — offshoots of some bigger group but with relatively few adherents. But at the bottom of it all, we can categorize most Christians into the two broad brands that hearken back to the days of Martin Luther and John Calvin — Catholics and Protestants. The latter broke away from the former centuries ago.

The word *Protestant* comes from the root *protest*, which is exactly what Luther and Calvin were doing. Even now, when you open up a prayer book in a Catholic church, you can read the official Catholic statement of hope that someday these disparate branches of Christianity will be reunited. But that hasn't happened. Almost 500 years after Luther posted his 95 Theses of protest against the Church in Wittenberg, Germany, the Christian U.S. — again, very broadly — remains split into those who continue to identify as part of the historic Roman Catholic Church and those who adhere to any of the thousands of Christian groups who are part of the breakaway movement.

Young people, I should point out, may not even recognize the word *Protestant*, a word that has apparently fallen out of favor. I'll discuss this phenomenon in more detail at the end of this chapter. For the purposes of this book, when I say *Protestant*, I'm referring to non-Catholic Christians — essentially dividing the Christian world into two groups based on whether they are Catholic or not.

Remember that the percentage of Americans who identify as Christian has gone down in recent decades as the percentage of those who don't have a formal religious identity has increased.

*This shrinkage of the Christian pie in the U.S. has resulted mainly from disappearing Protestants — even as Catholics have held their own.*

Gallup's research in 2009-2010 classified 55% of Americans in the non-Catholic Christian category. Back in the 1950s, that percentage was closer to 70%. But the percentage of American Catholics has remained relatively constant since the 1940s — at between about one-fifth to one-fourth of the population.

Here's what has happened:

- More Americans now than in the past don't give a religious identity when asked.

- That means, mathematically, that some religious identity group must be shrinking in size.

- Because America is largely a Christian nation, this shrinkage has occurred among Christians.

- Catholics have retained *their* share of America's religious pie over time, meaning that most of the shrinkage has occurred among Protestants.

The fact that the Protestant proportion of the U.S. population has been shrinking is not a new revelation. Two social scientists at the National Opinion Research Corporation (NORC) at the University of Chicago — Tom W. Smith and Seokho Kim — called the phenomenon "The Vanishing Protestant Majority" in their review of NORC's General Social Surveys data on the topic. Their analysis is complex, but Smith and Kim summarize it thusly: "An array of social forces from cohort turnover, to immigration, to reduced retention rates, indicate that the Protestant share of the population will continue to shrink and they will so lose their majority position in American society."

## HOW TO GROW A RELIGIOUS GROUP

### Internal Reproduction

Joseph Kennedy Sr. and his wife, Rose, had a large family — nine children. Mitt Romney and his wife, Ann, also have a large family — five children. These large families are no accident. The Kennedys were Catholic, and the Romneys are Mormon. Both of these religions historically have been very good at emphasizing *internal reproduction* among their members. The net result of Catholics and Mormons adhering to their faith's theologies has historically been large numbers of Catholic and Mormon babies.

Catholics have lost most of their big-family advantage today. Devout Catholics used to have many children because the Church discourages the use of artificial birth control. Catholic women increasingly ignore the "no birth control" part of their church's doctrine. In May 2012, we found that 82% of Catholics in the U.S. believed that birth control was morally acceptable.

Catholics are still slightly more likely to have large families than the national average. This slight fertility advantage is largely a result of Hispanic Catholics who represent a larger and larger part of the Catholic pie and who have more children. Catholics who are not Hispanic have fewer younger children than the national average or than Protestants. We are not seeing many Kennedy-style large non-Hispanic Catholic families anymore.

Mormon theological doctrine reinforces the value of having babies — lots of babies — giving Mormons a high rate of internal reproduction. And this works to their advantage in terms of growth. Here are some numbers: 49% of all Mormon adults have children in the home, compared with 41% of Catholics and 35% of Protestants.

Among Americans younger than 45, 37% of Mormons have three or more children, compared with 17% of Protestants, 21% of Catholics, and the overall national average of 17%.

These birth rates matter. Internal reproduction is not a trivial issue. Over time, birth rates can be a significant factor in the relative representation of a group in a population. Groups that have lots of children today have lots of adults tomorrow. Catholics and Mormons have historically enjoyed the fruit of this fertility equation.

Birth rates matter elsewhere around the world as well. One example comes from the Middle East. Over a span of decades, the ratio of Palestinians and Jews in Israel is going to be significantly affected by differences in the birth rates between these two groups, with the former having a higher fertility rate than the latter.

Protestants as a group have fallen behind Catholics and Mormons in terms of fertility, missing this clear and straightforward path to growth. Mainline Protestant groups such as Episcopalians in particular have a low rate of internal reproduction today. Episcopalians just don't have enough babies. Memo to Episcopalian leaders: Encourage your members to have more children, and your group will grow faster over time.

## Conversion

Young Mitt Romney spent two mission years in France attempting to convert residents of that predominantly Catholic nation to the Mormon faith. Erstwhile presidential candidate Jon Huntsman learned Mandarin Chinese and Taiwanese Hokkein while he was on his Mormon mission to Taiwan, a skill that was a big part of why President Barack Obama appointed him ambassador to China in 2009. The hit Broadway play *The Book of Mormon* is based on the adventures of Mormon missionaries in Uganda attempting to convert residents to their faith. All of this underscores another key way in which Mormons have tried to grow their numbers — *conversion.*

Protestant and Catholic groups historically have also attempted to convert non-Christians to their faith — including missionary work on foreign shores. I certainly have been no stranger to these efforts. A number of my Southern Baptist relatives were missionaries. My cousin and his wife spent a good part of their lives attempting to convert West Africans to Christianity. My mother's uncle spent his career as a medical missionary in China. Catholics over the centuries were able to convert huge numbers of people in the countries they colonized.

But we just don't see non-Mormon groups attempting to convert people to their religion today in the U.S. When is the last time a Baptist or Catholic missionary came to your door attempting to convert you to his or her faith? Protestants and Catholics alike have thus missed this path to growth in recent decades.

## In-migration

Religions can grow at a fast rate if large numbers of their adherents migrate into particular countries or regions. Protestants were the bulk of America's original immigrants — coming to this country searching for religious freedom to practice their faith. Thus, America was initially a largely Protestant immigrant nation. The problem for Protestants, however, is that fewer of their ilk have been migrating to this country in more recent times. Immigration into the U.S. from primarily Protestant countries has dried up.

On the other hand, many Catholics came into this country beginning in the late 1800s — mainly the huge in-migrations of adherents from southern Europe, and more recently, Catholic Hispanics from Mexico and Central and South America. This has been — and I emphasize *has been* — the key for Catholic growth in the U.S. over the last century and a half.

## How Not to Grow a Religious Group: Out-migration and Internal Losses

The relative size of a religious group is also affected by *out-migration*, or losses resulting from people leaving the population. These losses can be physical out-migration (for example, the percentage of Jews in Europe dropped in the 1930s and 1940s because of the rate of Jews leaving Europe) or people no longer identifying with a group. This is a problem for Catholics in the U.S. because a good deal of their younger non-Hispanic members leave the faith.

Another way to shrink a group is *internal losses*, or disproportionately high death rates. The percentage of the European population that was Jewish in the 1940s dropped dramatically because of the horribly high death rate perpetrated by the Holocaust.

## U.S. CATHOLICISM: SAVED BY HISPANICS

Head down to a local Catholic church some Sunday and sit in the back during Mass. It would not be unusual if you find yourself listening to a Spanish-speaking priest. This is in part because fewer and fewer young Anglo men make the decision to go into the priesthood. But the rise in Hispanic priests also reflects the fact that Catholics in this country are increasingly Hispanic — the result of the huge wave of Catholics from Mexico and Central and South America who have migrated into this country in recent years. This has allowed the Catholics to in essence "hold their own" population-wise — even as an increasing percentage of born-and-raised Catholics have abandoned their faith.

Catholics abandoning their faith? Didn't Newt Gingrich, raised as a Lutheran and a Baptist, quite publicly convert to Catholicism at the behest of his third wife, Callista? Yes he did, but this is a rare case. There are not a lot of Newt Gingriches around. This is symptomatic of a big problem facing Catholics. They lose lots of members who are raised Catholic but who abandon the faith when they grow up. And they gain relatively few converts. But the Catholic gains from immigration have more than made up for their internal losses.

Changes in immigration patterns have huge implications for the American economy and are a big issue in American politics. Now we see that they also have implications for American religion.

Patterns of immigration into this country are changing once again, however. The in-migration of Spanish-speaking Catholics is slowing down. One recent study showed that the number of Mexicans immigrating into the U.S. dropped by 60% between 2006 and 2010. And Mexicans — most of whom are Catholics — are by far the biggest source of recent immigrants into the U.S. The future size of the Catholic church in the U.S., in short, could be in jeopardy — subject to a slow shrinkage in the years ahead as its most plentiful source of new members dries up.

All is not doom and gloom for the future of the Catholic church. As a result of *past* migration patterns, the population of Hispanic Catholics already in the U.S. is disproportionately young. Forty-five percent of American Catholics aged 18 to 29 in Gallup's surveys are Hispanic, along with nearly one-third of those aged 30 to 49. That compares with 18% of Catholics aged 50 to 64 and 12% of those 65 and older who are Hispanic.

*This means that the Catholic church in the U.S. will tilt more and more Hispanic in the years ahead. Aging white Catholics will increasingly go to church alongside large numbers of young Hispanic Catholics.* And as these older white Catholics die off, they will be replaced by an increasingly Hispanic cohort of younger Catholics. The good news for the Catholic church is that Hispanics have a higher fertility rate than non-Hispanics. Hispanic Catholics younger than 40 will reproduce and replace themselves at a higher than normal rate.

Thus, the Catholic church should be the net beneficiary of the fact that young Hispanic Catholics and the children of Hispanic Catholics who have entered this country in recent decades will have many children. Assuming that these children remain Catholic — which seems to be the case based on Gallup's data to date — this fecundity will bring many new Catholics into the system from within, even as the supply of new Catholics from without slows down.

## U.S. PROTESTANTISM: MUSICAL CHAIRS

It is clear that Protestants have been the big losers in the American religion game in recent years. Their ranks have shrunk on a proportionate basis even as their Christian competitors, the Catholics, have held their own.

Basically, Protestants have done everything wrong over the decades in terms of their growth. There have been no recent great waves of Protestant immigrants into this country. Protestants already in this country are not having babies at a particularly prolific rate. Protestants are not attracting large numbers of converts from non-Protestant religions. And Protestants are not living longer than non-Protestants. Hence, Protestants have continued to shrink as a percentage of the U.S. population.

The only saving grace for Protestantism, it seems to me, is its protean nature — the amazing ability of Protestants to morph and shape themselves into new and newer groups that in theory can be directly in tune with the needs and benefits that their prospective parishioners desire. Protestant groups come in many ever-changing varieties. Protestant parishioners have the unique ability to move around from Protestant group to Protestant group without significant disruptions to their basic faith patterns.

## Thousands of Brands

Beer drinkers have benefited from the rise of microbreweries — those small brewers of beer that are helping fragment the beer industry and that provide beer drinkers with many different types of beer to choose from. In similar fashion, there are many, many "microdenominations" under the Protestant umbrella — providing numerous different types of Protestant churches to choose from. This in theory is a good thing for the marketing of Protestantism.

When you think about Protestant religions in this country, you probably think of the big broad Protestant groups — Episcopalians,

Presbyterians, Baptists, and Methodists. But keep in mind that these large groups are only a small slice of the Protestant pie. Protestantism today — still the largest religious group in the U.S. by far — is much like a Russian nesting doll puzzle where the top of each doll can be removed to show another smaller doll underneath.

Take Jane Smith — a hypothetical American Protestant woman. She could first be classified as a Christian. She then could be further classified as a non-Catholic Christian. So far, so good. But then Ms. Smith would need further classification. Her broad denominational identity could be subdivided into a smaller denomination. Then perhaps even a still smaller denomination. So, Ms. Jane Smith could be classified as a Christian, and then as a non-Catholic Christian, and then as a Baptist, and then as a Southern Baptist, and then as a Southern Baptist who is affiliated with the Cooperative Baptist Fellowship, and so on.

The 54% of Americans who are Protestants, in short, can be subdivided into thousands of specific brands of Christianity. Almost every Protestant denomination in the U.S. can be subdivided and subdivided again, creating an ever-expanding group of religious brands.

Protestants in the United States thus form a fascinating and unusual religious category. Unlike the case with Catholics, Jews, Muslims, Hindus, or Buddhists, the term *Protestant* is not a distinct religious identity. It's a general term used to describe the huge number of slices of the non-Catholic Christian pie.

In fact, no one knows precisely how many Protestant groups there are. Some sources say there are more than 30,000 different types of Christian groups worldwide, although this calculation totally depends on how fine-tuned one's definition of a distinct group is. Most people recognize the wide-ranging varieties of non-Catholic Christians that have the longest history and the most members: Baptists, Methodists, Lutherans, Episcopalians, and Presbyterians. These broad labels are, however, just that — broad.

There are many different specific branches *within* each of these groupings, including at least 50 different types of Baptist groups alone. The Hartford Institute for Religion Study lists hundreds of denominational websites in the U.S. Even as I write this, I'm reading a news story about the creation of still another Presbyterian offshoot — the Evangelical Covenant Order, or ECO. The Southern Baptist denomination in which I was raised itself has split, with more moderate Southern Baptists moving to the Cooperative Baptist Fellowship, while conservative, fundamentalist members stayed with the original denomination. In fact, the Southern Baptist denomination, the largest single Protestant denomination in the U.S., will most likely continue to split, morph, and dissolve into smaller groups of Baptists in the years to come. This is quite natural; Southern Baptists themselves split off from larger groups of Baptists back before the Civil War.

Plus, some of the fastest growing and largest types of Protestant groups in the U.S. are "nondenominational" or "Christians with no further names" — groups without a classic religious identity.

## Religious Switching

This great diversity of religious groups in the U.S. is a big deal because it leads to the uniquely American phenomenon of "religious switching." This is the process by which individuals choose different religious identities than the ones they grew up with as they move through life.

I wrote a detailed analysis of this fascinating process a few years back in an article called "The Religious Switcher in the United States," published in the *American Sociological Review.* One key finding: Switching religions is particularly easy to do in the U.S. because of what I've been talking about — the large number of different religious "products" to choose from and because there are not major doctrinal differences between Protestant denominations.

When it comes to brand loyalty, marketers like to distinguish between products or services that are difficult to change and those that are easy to change. Banks and cell phone service providers, your electrical company, and your primary care doctor are examples of products and services that are more difficult to change. On the other hand, your preferred brand of cereal, your car, or your grocery store are quite easy to change. American religion — compared with religions around the world — fits more into the latter "easy to change" category than the former.

Think about restaurants in this country. You do not lack for a wide variety of dining choices. Restaurateurs are constantly coming up with new ideas for food options, price points, mechanisms for getting the food to their customers, and other hooks to get you into their establishments. If you don't like McDonald's, then you can go to Five Guys for your hamburgers. If you don't like Five Guys, head on over to Wendy's where they are morphing their hamburgers into something new. If you don't like Wendy's, go to Burger King — and so forth. This wide variety of "brand choices" in the dining industry helps keep the industry vibrant. Even as I write this, the venerable department story J.C. Penney has announced it is totally morphing itself into a big store with less discounting and dozens of small "boutiques" within each store — under the assumption that more choices means more customers.

These examples of the competitive nature of the capitalist, free enterprise system are similar to the wide variety of "brand choices" within Protestantism. Entrepreneurs who create new product choices from which consumers can choose, the theory goes, help sustain a vibrant and growth-oriented economy. Religious leaders who create new Protestant denominations can similarly help sustain religious vibrancy and growth. This is not an original thought on my part. Some scholars think this ease of switching among religious groups is one of the reasons why America has stayed more religious than dominantly one-religion countries of Europe.

And there is a lot of switching going on. Back in the 1970s, I found that about 25% to 32% of Americans had changed religions. More recently, the Pew Research Center found that more than four in 10 Americans had changed religions at some point in their lives.

This religious switching has produced a different Protestant landscape in the U.S. from what we would have seen decades ago. First, as I have reviewed, more and more Americans have switched to no religious identity at all — even if they remained religious. We see more evidence of this shift out of "branded religions" when we look at the types of Protestant religions that are growing. Fewer and fewer Americans identify with traditional mainline Protestant denominations. Episcopalians, Presbyterians, Methodists, and other mainline denominations are shrinking. More and more

Americans have switched to a nondenominational Christian identity. Nondenominational Christian churches, evangelical and rigorous fundamentalist groups, and those individuals who simply choose to call themselves "Christian" without any allegiance to a specific denomination or other religious group are growing.

This table shows changes over the past 45 years or so, based on Gallup data. All of these Protestant denominations have lost ground size-wise. The relative number of Methodists and Presbyterians has in fact dropped in half since 1967.

**Changes in Identification With Protestant Denominations**

|              | 1967 | 1998 | 2009 | 2010 |
|--------------|------|------|------|------|
| Methodist    | 14%  | 9%   | 7%   | 7%   |
| Presbyterian | 6%   | 3%   | 3%   | 3%   |
| Episcopalian | 3%   | 2%   | 2%   | 2%   |
| Lutheran     | 8%   | 5%   | 5%   | 5%   |
| Baptist      | 21%  | 19%  | 16%  | 17%  |

In addition to these changes, as I have mentioned, more Americans today simply label themselves as "Christian," with no further distinction. This marks another big change in religious identity in the U.S. — *the increasing tendency among Protestants to say they are Christian but without specific denominational identification.*

Another important source of information about shifting religious identification comes from the American Religious Identification Survey (ARIS) conducted by researchers at Trinity College in Hartford, Connecticut. The ARIS project confirms an increase from 1990 to 2008 in the percentage of Americans who simply say "Christian" when asked to name their religion — rather than a specific denominational name. Plus, the ARIS study shows an increase in those who are classified as "nondenominational" and confirms the decline in the percentage of Americans who identify as Baptists, Methodists, Lutherans, Presbyterians, and Episcopalians.

Basically, Americans who are Christian and not Catholic increasingly seem to dislike labels. Protestants have redefined themselves in the U.S., tending more and more to group themselves into the "nondenominational" or "Christians with no further names" groups and less and less to retain identification with classic mainline Christian groups. In addition, some former Protestants are now within the group of "nones" I discussed earlier.

Some of these new unbranded entities are the so-called "megachurches." These nondenominational Protestant churches are relatively nonhierarchal, not controlled by any central authority, and focused on providing a wide variety of functions for their members.

As I noted previously, many years ago, my mother's uncle set out as a medical missionary to China. His mission work was carried out completely within the purview of the Southern Baptist Convention's Foreign Mission Board (now the International Mission Board), which trained, sponsored, and supported him. My cousin's wife is today similarly focused on mission work in French-speaking West Africa. She, like my mother's uncle, was raised a Southern Baptist. But her mission work is now being sponsored by and supported by — not the Southern Baptist's International Mission Board — but a single megachurch in North Texas. This megachurch is so "mega" that it can afford to set up its own mission work overseas and has to publish a directory on its website for its campus, which spreads over acres like a small community college. Many of the members of this congregation no doubt used to be Southern Baptists, like my cousin's wife. Today they are "Christian" with no further designation. This same pattern has been duplicated across the country.

Many scholars have asked the question of why Americans are abandoning more formal mainline denominations — with many different answers.

Mainline denominations may not be providing the benefits that worshipers want. Many offer a place for worship on Sunday, a setting for weddings and funerals, and not much more. Some of these traditional denominations may be so focused on doctrine and church politics — for example, the Southern Baptist denomination's focus on biblically literal doctrinal beliefs and the Episcopal church's wrenching debates about ordaining gay clergy — that there is little time left to focus on the benefits that their members desire.

Today's high-growth nondenominational churches, on the other hand, don't have to worry about denominational matters. They can focus on providing members with a host of social benefits: friendship groups (increasingly important in an anomic, "bowling-alone" society), outings, activities, affinity groups, recreational opportunities, and study groups.

In addition, there are "true believer" issues. American Christians may also be seeking faiths that challenge them personally (i.e., those that have a relatively high cost of membership), while providing a close relationship to an active God who provides guidance in daily life. Religious groups that demand more from their members are more successful in retaining them. Marines, fraternities, Navy SEALs, and other groups with difficult entrance rituals have long known that those who survive initiation hardships can be fanatically loyal. Some religious groups have apparently successfully adopted the same philosophy — and in similar fashion, have found that tougher membership standards can increase member adherence.

Some churches and denominations get more out of their members than others. More active members signify more dynamic and growing religious entities. The groups with the highest member participation — Mormons, evangelicals, Pentecostals, nondenominational Christians — are growing the fastest. Groups whose members are less active, including Episcopalians, simply aren't exciting their members, and their growth is essentially stagnant.

Jews and the mainline denominations — Episcopalians, Lutherans, Methodists, and Presbyterians — are, by a measure of membership "yield," the least religious groups in America today. Those who identify with these groups are less likely to go to religious services. More fundamentalist and nondenominational groups — where the growth is — have the most active members; in other words, they have the highest member church attendance "yield." The yield measure is a good indicator of vibrancy and growth.

Finally, it's worth noting that we are all clearly becoming less hierarchical and more ad hoc in much of what we do. Bottom-up, nonhierarchical movements are thriving. Traditional hierarchies are in danger of becoming passé. Think about the Arab Spring and the rise in social media. Think about how communication has evolved away from "big media" and focused more on "small media," including micro Internet sites, Facebook postings, and in particular individually originated Twitter feeds. Everything is moving toward less hierarchy and more informal, flat, ad hoc organizing. Protestant religions appear to be no exception.

## THE MYSTERIOUS CASE OF THE DISAPPEARING PROTESTANTS

What if I asked you if you are a Protestant? If you are a non-Catholic Christian 60 or older, the chances are high that you will say "yes." If you are a non-Catholic Christian younger than 40, the chances are higher that you will say "no." That's because the word *Protestant* appears to be losing its identity and relevance with younger Americans. *Americans who by all of the usual measures qualify as being Protestant now appear less likely to recognize or use that word to describe themselves.*

I looked carefully at those we classify in our surveys as *either* "Protestant" *or* "other Christian." Some respondents identify themselves as Protestant right off the bat when asked. Some instead called themselves "other Christians" — those who initially identified not as Protestant, nor Catholic, but as some other religion. And then, after further questioning, these people agreed that their "other" religion was Christian.

Of this total non-Catholic Christian group, 53% identified with the word *Protestant*, while 47% did not (and ended up being classified as "other Christian"). I looked at the split between these two groups on a percentage basis by age. The results show a dramatic pattern. The younger the non-Catholic Christian, the more likely he or she is to be an "other Christian." The older the non-Catholic Christian, the more likely he or she is to be a "Protestant."

The lost relevance of the word *Protestant* has to do with labels, not what is underneath the label. The word *Protestant* is not for the most part an "official" term. It is not the formal name of any specific religious group as far as I know. It derives from the original Protestant Reformation, which in turn derived from the fact that this reformation was based on a "protest" against Roman Catholicism. The term *Protestant* is a catchall title that Christians today simply are less likely to recognize or use to identify themselves, particularly younger Americans; many prefer instead to simply call themselves *Christians*.

I'm not sure why this is the case. But given these trends, it's a reasonable conjecture that the term *Protestant* could disappear altogether over the next number of years. The word has simply gone out of fashion. Fewer Americans will talk about being a *Protestant*, and fewer will use the term.

## Bottom Line

Americans have become more likely to say they have no religious identity in recent decades. Americans who do claim a religious identity increasingly say it's "Christian," without naming a specific denomination. More and more Americans identify with unbranded, nondenominational religions. Membership in classic, traditional, and standard churches has declined. Other forms of worship have arisen to take their place.

Even as more Americans say they don't have a religious identity, other indicators of religiousness have been stable over time. We are witnessing more of a shift in *how* Americans express their religiousness rather than a decrease in religiousness per se.

The shift to a more free-form, unbranded religiousness in America will have several consequences in the years ahead, including continuing troubles for traditional Protestant denominations. We have already witnessed a substantial decline in the percentage of Americans who identify with "regular" Protestant denominations. These denominations are getting hammered from a number of perspectives. The main problems for traditional Protestant groups today: Their members have fewer babies; they don't have substantial conversion rates; and most important, they don't have an inflow of Protestant immigrants into the country.

We can expect to see continuing shrinking of the traditional Protestant denominations that once counted among their members the significant majority of all Americans. This includes the mainline denominations that are bastions for upscale white Americans and the very large Baptist denominations. The numbers of Southern Baptists, still the single largest religious group in America other than the Roman Catholic Church, have already been shrinking. One recent president of the Southern Baptist Convention said that half of all Southern Baptist churches may close by 2030.

Despite all of the many brands to choose from and the ease of switching from one brand to another, Protestants as a group have been shrinking. Obviously, the unique nature of Protestantism in America today hasn't stopped this process. And I'm not sure I see much on the horizon that is going to change that. Maybe the number of Protestants would have shrunk even further without their ability to morph and change — like the advertising agency that tells a client with decreasing sales that sales would have fallen much more rapidly without the advertising agency's help.

If there is growth among non-Catholic Christians, it will come from the more free-form, nondenominational groups or from even more casual groups of Protestants who get together to worship. The mighty megachurches that draw thousands of worshippers will grow, even as nearby Episcopal, Methodist, Presbyterian, Lutheran, and Baptist churches desperately search for members.

The word *Protestant* itself will likely fade away. Young people simply don't use the word to identify themselves today.

The Catholic church has been saved by immigration and birth rates. A significant portion of immigrants to the U.S. in recent decades have been Catholic. The result is a substantial Hispanic skew in today's younger Catholics. An astounding 45% of Catholics younger than 30 are Hispanic. These younger Hispanics seem to be hanging on to their Catholicism. The fact that almost half of young Catholics are Hispanic shows just what trouble the Catholic church in America would be in if not for Hispanic immigration. The Catholic church will continue to be rescued by the fruits of immigration in the years ahead because this large group of young Hispanic Catholics will have many children of their own.

Right now, we don't see any signs of an unusual increase in non-Christian religions. Christianity will prevail in the U.S. America will remain very much a Christian nation in the decades ahead, albeit less so than in the past because of an increase in Americans who don't have a religious identity.

Other than their religious identity, Americans remain underneath it all remarkably religious, and I expect that they will continue to be so in the years ahead. There is a latent religiosity in the American public. But how this latent religiosity percolates to the surface has changed and will continue to change in the years ahead. And as I continue, I'll look at many of the ways in which this will occur.

# CHAPTER III

## Religion Is Good for Your Health

Religious Americans are healthier and happier than those who are not religious. This finding is important because it potentially connects with one of the major social and economic problems of our time — a hugely expensive healthcare system with costs that reflect in part the nation's unhealthy lifestyle choices. Religious Americans exhibit more of the types of behaviors that those interested in the health and wellbeing of the nation want to encourage. If Americans were to become more religious, it is quite possible they would be happier and healthier, and the cost of healthcare in this country would decline.

The explanations for this relationship are not yet fully understood. It's fairly clear that becoming religious may cause people to be happier and to feel better. And it's a reasonable, although not totally proven assumption, that becoming religious may lead to better health.

Despite the enduring controversy that usually surrounds matters of religion and public policy, those entrusted with improving wellbeing and health outcomes and lowering health costs will eventually have to focus on taking advantage of the widely confirmed religion-health connection. Average Americans, seeking ways to improve their health and wellbeing, may also increasingly turn to religion for these same reasons. The apparent power of religion to help achieve one of the nation's most important social and fiscal goals — increasing wellbeing and lowering healthcare costs — will be too significant to ignore.

## NORMAN VINCENT PEALE WAS ON TO SOMETHING

Norman Vincent Peale, the longtime minister at the Marble Collegiate Church in New York, wrote his famous book *The Power of Positive Thinking* in 1952. To date, it has sold more than 7 million copies. The basic premise of the book is clear from the title. Much of what Peale talks about is the power of religion to relieve suffering and worry. As he says in the introduction, "How can I be so certain that the practice of these principles will produce such results? The answer is simply that for many years in the Marble Collegiate Church of New York City we have taught a system of creative living based on spiritual techniques, carefully noting its operation in the lives of hundreds of people." Note the reference to "spiritual techniques."

Not everyone liked Peale's book, no doubt because it attempted to straddle the line between two very complex areas, religion and psychology. Psychologists and other mental health professionals attacked the book because it lacked rigorous, empirical research. Peale's suppositions and recommendations were not based on science but on his observations and the testimony of people he came in contact with. I remember my father making light of my mother's interest in Peale's book, presumably because it was considered to be "theology light." My mother was much more of a positive thinker and enjoyed her life more than my father, a professional theologian who tended to look at life through a jaundiced, more negative lens. So the book may well have been effective for her regardless of its lack of theological rigor.

Peale died in 1993 at the age of 95. He would probably be thinking even more positively these days if he were still alive. The data we are accumulating show that he was on to something. The type of positive relationship between religion and freedom from worry that Peale discussed is increasingly backed up by hard-nosed evidence.

## RELIGION, WELLBEING, AND HEALTH

My colleagues Dan Witters and Sangeeta Agrawal and I conducted a series of analyses on the relationship between religion and wellbeing and health, based on more than 676,000 Gallup-Healthways Well-Being Index interviews conducted in 2010 and 2011. The results, in the broadest possible terms, confirm that Americans who are the most religious also have the highest levels of wellbeing — across a number of dimensions.

The term *wellbeing* is general and a little ambiguous. Gallup defines wellbeing using six components of the Gallup-Healthways Well-Being Index: overall life evaluation, emotional health, physical health, healthy behaviors, work environment, and access to basic wellbeing necessities. The overall Gallup-Healthways Well-Being Index composite score summarizes how Americans rate on this series of measures.

For the purposes of this analysis, we based our assessment of Americans' relative degree of religiousness on their responses to two questions about the importance of religion and church attendance. This yields three specific groups:

1. **Very religious** — Religion is an important part of daily life; members of this group attend church/synagogue/mosque at least every week or almost every week. This group constitutes 41% of the adult population.

2. **Nonreligious** — Religion is not an important part of daily life; members of this group seldom or never attend church/synagogue/mosque. This group constitutes 31% of the adult population.

3. **Moderately religious** — All others who do not fall into the very religious or nonreligious groups but who gave valid responses on both religion questions are classified as moderately religious. This group constitutes 28% of the adult population.

As we see throughout this book, Americans' religiousness is related to age, gender, race and ethnicity, region and state of the country, socio-economic status, marital status, and child-bearing status. Wellbeing is also related to these variables. We statistically controlled for all of these background and demographic variables for this analysis. Our results reflect the relationship between religiousness and wellbeing *after* all of these other factors are taken into account.

The average score on the Well-Being Index for Americans who are very religious is 69.2. The average is 65.3 for those who are nonreligious. That's a 3.9-point difference, which is highly statistically significant given the large sample sizes. The difference between very religious and moderately religious is even larger, at 5.5 points. These differences would have occurred by chance alone only very infrequently. **Bottom line:** *Americans who are the most religious have the highest wellbeing.*

The accompanying table shows the breakdown by religiousness for each of the six sub-indexes of the Gallup-Healthways Well-Being Index. Very religious Americans enjoy higher scores across all six of the key wellbeing areas compared with moderately religious Americans and higher scores across five of the wellbeing areas compared with nonreligious Americans.

### Gallup-Healthways Well-Being Index Domain Scores by Religiosity

Controlling for age, gender, race and ethnicity, region and state of the country, socio-economic status, marital status, and child-bearing status

| Index | Very religious | Moderately religious | Nonreligious |
|---|---|---|---|
| Life Evaluation | 53.3 | 44.8 | 48.6 |
| Emotional Health | 81.9 | 76.3 | 77.6 |
| Physical Health | 77.5 | 74.2 | 78.1 |
| Healthy Behaviors | 68.3 | 61.5 | 59.1 |
| Work Environment | 50.6 | 45.8 | 45.8 |
| Basic Access | 83.5 | 79.6 | 82.7 |

## Religious Americans Are Less Depressed

The impact of depression on Americans' lives and on the economy is enormous. The National Institute of Mental Health estimates that major depressive disorders affect 7% of the adult population in any given year. Gallup data show that 17% of Americans have been diagnosed with depression at some point in their lives.

We don't know the exact causes and, in particular, the cure for depression. But we know that very religious Americans are less likely to report that they have been diagnosed with depression than those who are moderately religious or nonreligious. This relationship between depression and religion — again, based on an analysis of more than 676,000 Gallup-Healthways Well-Being Index interviews — is statistically significant after controlling for major demographic and regional variables.

The statistical estimates are that nearly one in six (15.1%) very religious American adults has been diagnosed with depression. For those who are moderately religious and nonreligious, the numbers are higher: 20.5% and 17.4%, respectively.

Gallup asks Americans if they have *ever* been diagnosed with depression by a nurse or doctor. On the other hand, Gallup's measure of religiousness is based on asking Americans to indicate how religious they are *at the time of the interview*. This means we are correlating a contemporaneous measure of religiousness with a lifetime cumulative measure of depression. For these and other reasons, we can't say that the act of becoming religious will reduce or eliminate depression for those currently experiencing it. It could be, for example, that depressed people don't go to church precisely because they are depressed. Maybe they don't want to leave the house. Nevertheless, the data show a significant connection between these two attributes and certainly suggest the strong possibility that being religious helps ward off depression.

## Don't Worry, Be Religious

Remember "Don't Worry, Be Happy" — the title of the popular song by Bobby McFerrin? It looks like we should be singing a new song: "Don't Worry, Be Religious."

Gallup asked Americans if they experienced worry, stress, sadness, or anger during the day preceding the interview. Again, we find a statistically significant relationship with religiousness and these emotions. Very religious Americans are less likely to be worried or to experience stress or anger than their moderately religious and nonreligious counterparts. Only with sadness is there no difference between the very religious and those who are nonreligious.

**Negative Daily Affect: Emotions Experienced "A lot of the day yesterday"**

Controlling for age, income, education, gender, race/ethnicity, marital status, and region

| Degree of Religiousness | Worry | Stress | Sadness | Anger |
|---|---|---|---|---|
| Very religious | 28.6% | 35.8% | 16.2% | 11.3% |
| Nonreligious | 33.0% | 43.8% | 16.1% | 15.1% |
| Moderately religious | 37.1% | 44.0% | 21.6% | 16.2% |

About 36% of very religious Americans experienced stress the day before the interview compared with 44% of moderately religious and nonreligious Americans. You are about 30% more likely to worry if you are moderately religious than if you are very religious, 33% more likely to experience sadness, and 43% more likely to experience anger. Religion is certainly not a cure-all for worry and stress, but it certainly appears to have a measureable effect.

The conclusion that religion is related to wellbeing gains more support the more scientists look into it. Positive relationships between religiosity and subjective wellbeing and health have been very well-documented. As social scientists Chaeyoon Lim and Robert Putnam said, "Numerous studies find religion to be closely related to life satisfaction and happiness." A few years ago, two psychologists, Christopher Peterson and Martin Seligman, compiled a long list of character virtues that research data show are associated with being more religious — including quality of family life; lower levels of marital conflict; and higher levels of forgiveness, compassion, pro-social values, happiness, life purpose, psychological wellbeing, life satisfaction, coping with illness and psychosocial stress, and coping.

Princeton's Angus Deaton has explored these same relationships in Gallup data from around the world and finds the same basic patterns. Deaton summarizes his findings as follows: "An overall summary of these results is that, controlling for age, education, and sex, religion is generally beneficial for health and for health-related personal and social behaviors."

## Not Specific to One Religion

This relationship between religiousness and wellbeing occurs among Americans of all faiths. It's not exclusive to any religion. Very religious Jews, Mormons, Muslims, Catholics, Protestants, and those who identify with other non-Christian religions have higher wellbeing than those in each of these religious groups who are moderately religious or nonreligious. In fact, even those who are very religious but do not have a formal religious identity have higher wellbeing than do their respective counterparts who are moderately religious or nonreligious.

All of this establishes — rather remarkably — the existence of a correlation between religion and subjective wellbeing. Correlation is no proof of causation, of course. I'll return to that issue — after a look at the fascinating relationship between religiousness and health.

## Religion Correlated With Better Health

A key part of the Gallup-Healthways Well-Being Index is the measure of healthy behaviors. It turns out that the differences in our health by degree of religiousness are quite large. Very religious Americans' self-reports of not smoking, eating healthy foods, eating fruits and vegetables, and exercising are all higher than among the rest of the population. There is a 9.2-point difference on the composite Healthy Behaviors Index score between the very religious and the nonreligious group — with the most religious Americans scoring 68.3 compared with 59.1 for the nonreligious. This relationship is highly statistically significant.

You may have read about experiments in which researchers ask people at remote locations to pray for a sick person — with the researchers then following up to see if the sick person gets better. That's not the type of relationship between religion and health I'm talking about here. Nor am I talking about the power of religion and positive thinking to help cure disease on the part of the individual who has the disease. I am talking about the fact that people who are the most religious appear to engage in healthier behaviors compared with those who are moderately or not at all religious. As Deaton summarizes it, there is a "large contemporaneous empirical literature that documents that religious people typically have better health outcomes."

Smoking stands out as the single behavior that most differentiates the very religious from less religious Americans, making it worth looking at in more detail. Nonreligious Americans are more than twice as likely to be smokers than those who are very religious — 26.4% compared with 12.5%.

This is an important finding. Smoking is well-established as a controllable behavior that has a huge impact on health costs in the U.S. The Centers for Disease Control and Prevention estimates that smoking costs almost $200 billion a year in healthcare costs and lost productivity. One in five deaths in the U.S. are tobacco-related.

Smoking is correlated with a number of demographic characteristics, including: gender (men smoke more than women), education and income (less well-educated Americans and Americans with lower incomes are the most likely to smoke), age (younger Americans are more likely to smoke than older Americans), and region (Southerners are most likely to smoke).

These demographic variables are also related to religiousness — as we will see in the forthcoming chapters. Women are more religious than men, older people are more religious than younger people, and Southerners are more religious than those living elsewhere in the country. So there is a lot of "confounding" among these variables. But statistically, when we control for gender, age, and region (along with the other variables), the difference in smoking rates by religiousness persists. In other words, a poor, young, never-graduated-from-high-school Southerner who is religious is less likely to smoke than the same type of person who is not religious.

Taken at face value, the data suggest that if everyone in America suddenly became very religious, the overall adult smoking rate in the U.S. would be 12.5%. That's a major drop from the current 21% who smoke. Of course, there is more to smoking than just religiousness. But clearly, being religious is somehow associated with avoiding the smoking habit.

## THE ISSUE OF CAUSALITY

Millions of Americans get out of bed and drink coffee each morning. At almost the same time, the sun rises in the East. Would we be correct to assume that consumption of coffee causes the sun to rise? On a yearly basis, sales of ice cream and drowning deaths are highly correlated. Should we then assume that consumption of ice cream causes drowning deaths? No. In each situation, the two events are correlated with one another. But the correlation does not imply that one of the events *causes* the other. If Americans quit drinking coffee, the sun would still rise. If people quit buying ice cream in the summer, drowning deaths would still be high (because people are most likely to swim in the summer).

In terms of religion and health, we have seen that highly religious Americans have higher wellbeing and are healthier than those who are less religious. But this does not prove that religiousness per se causes or leads to better health. Correlation is not proof of causation.

People like to claim that taking certain vitamins or drugs or undergoing certain medical procedures results in better health. But often it's difficult to prove that one causes the other when rigorous, controlled, experimental studies are conducted. Parents take their kids with runny noses and coughs to the doctor. Their kids get better a couple of days later. Did the doctor help? Not necessarily. Most colds get better on their own.

Much of the existing data demonstrating the relationship between religiosity, wellbeing, and health is cross-sectional. We take a group of people at one point in time and see if those who score higher on one dimension tend to score higher on another dimension. But, as my examples attest, this doesn't mean that high scores on one dimension actually *cause* higher scores on the other dimension. The most religious people in a population are also the happiest and the healthiest. It certainly seems logical that being religious causes one to have higher wellbeing and to have better health outcomes. But we don't know that for sure.

One way to get at the causality issue is to control for regional and demographic variables, which is exactly what we have done with the Gallup data. The relationship between religion, wellbeing, and health persists even with these controls in place. The results increase the chances that religion is causing better wellbeing and health but don't prove it.

What else could be driving the relationship between religion and wellbeing? It could be that certain people — defined by their genetics or demographic characteristics — are the types of people who seek out religion *and* who engage in healthy behaviors.

- Let's say, for example, that there is a certain gene that gives people a personality predisposition for a high happiness set point. It's possible that this same gene could cause people to be spiritual and interested in getting together with other groups of people. In this instance, the gene would be the cause behind both wellbeing and religiousness.

- Or perhaps people who live in certain cities or regions are generally happier and also generally more religious. Living in these areas could cause high levels on both dimensions.

- Maybe people who work hard to be healthy have a lot of energy, and this energy spills over into their decision to take time for religion. Or people who are healthy could feel better about themselves, and this in turn could lead them to be more open to or predisposed to the acceptance of religion.

- Or maybe certain types of people have genes that predispose them to be slothful, lazy, and to have addictive personalities — and maybe these genes in turn lead these people to overeat, smoke, and drink and to decide not to take the time and effort to be religious.

Unfortunately, it's hard to test these possibilities. It would be nice to have controlled experimental studies in which people are assigned to different treatment conditions or panel studies, which follow the same people over time.

But we don't have many experimental studies. We have a hard time in social science randomly assigning real people to various treatment groups and then following them over time. For our research purposes, it would be great — scientifically speaking — to randomly choose 10,000 people and force them to become very religious and randomly choose another 10,000 people and force them to be nonreligious — and then follow them throughout their lives to monitor the differences. Alas, we have not been able to figure out how to accomplish this. For the most part, we haven't been able to conduct a religiously oriented version of the famous Framingham Heart Study, which followed the residents of Framingham, Massachusetts, for decades, tracking their health. Unfortunately, religiousness was not one of the variables the Framingham researchers tracked over the years.

Still, some good news came in 2010 from social scientists Chaeyoon Lim and Robert Putnam, who were able to follow the Framingham model in relationship to religion on a much shorter term basis. They analyzed data from a longitudinal panel study that followed the same people across time. They tracked in particular people who changed their religion — and looked carefully at changes in life satisfaction and religiousness. They found evidence of a direct causal path between higher levels of religiousness and life satisfaction. The authors said, "Our findings suggest that religious people are more satisfied with their lives because they regularly attend religious services and build social networks in their congregations." This means that increased religiousness, particularly church participation, increases wellbeing. Other researchers, using different panel studies, have similarly concluded that religious service attendance does appear to result in increased happiness.

There is thus a growing sense among researchers that the link between religiousness and subjective wellbeing is direct and causal. Something about being religious, or becoming more religious, helps people have higher wellbeing.

Health is a slightly different matter. The correlation between religion and good health is well-established, as we have seen in the Gallup data. Other studies have found similar results. A study by researchers at the National Center for Health Statistics concluded: "In a nationwide cohort of Americans, predominantly Christians, analyses demonstrated a lower risk of death independent of confounders among those reporting religious attendance at least weekly compared to never."

Wellbeing in general is correlated with positive health outcomes. This relationship is robust and has been demonstrated repeatedly in multiple studies. Because religiousness causes wellbeing, and because wellbeing is related to health, it's seems logical and reasonable that religiousness causes better health. But we are not yet at the point where we can say this positively. In scientific terms, we hypothesize that becoming more religious will have a salubrious impact on one's health. I think there is good evidence that the data support this hypothesis. As good researchers, of course, we continue to look for more evidence to shed light on this hypothesis.

## EXPLANATIONS FOR THE RELIGIOUSNESS-WELLBEING-HEALTH CONNECTION

What is behind the relationship between religiousness and higher levels of wellbeing and health? Here are three explanations:

1.  **Many religions either explicitly or implicitly promote norms of behavior that are in turn associated with higher wellbeing and healthy behavior.** Behaviors that lead to bad physical health outcomes — including smoking and excessive drinking — are normatively less acceptable in many religions' cultures. I grew up in a Southern Baptist tradition in which it was very much a no-no to smoke or drink liquor. Mormons are in general fairly strongly admonished to seek pleasure from reinforcers other than caffeine, alcohol, or nicotine. Many other religions focus on sources of positive reinforcement and happiness that do not depend on the type of external stimuli provided by alcohol, nicotine, and gluttonous eating. If a person begins to worship frequently within the framework of one of these types of religions, that person is more likely to adopt these norms and therefore, is more likely to be healthy.

2. **Religions by definition include a belief in God or a higher power. That belief can provide comfort, surcease from sorrow, and inner spiritual calmness.** Many religions provide explanations for life's traumas, negative experiences, and bad things. Many also focus on belief in an afterlife and faith that earthly sorrow will be rectified after death. All this can increase wellbeing, mental health, and acceptance and help prevent depression and negative emotions. Loneliness, dwelling on problems, jealousy, and feeling blameful may be less likely to occur among individuals who are highly religious. And that in turn is related to more positive wellbeing outcomes.

3. **Active participation in a religious community provides individuals with friends, fellow worshippers, social networks, and social support.** This may be one of the most important causes for the positive wellbeing and health outcomes among highly religious people. The research by Putnam and Lim reinforces the hypothesis that social support — defined as friendship networks within the church — coupled with a strong religious identity, cause higher life satisfaction. Higher life satisfaction and wellbeing in turn lead to higher levels of physical health. A great deal of research shows that friends and relationships are correlated with longevity. Putnam and Lim argue that friends and relationships within the context of a church or religious body may be "supercharged friends" — more important than secular friends and relationships.

The challenge of figuring out the exact role of these three types of processes in mediating the connection between religion, wellbeing, and health lies ahead of us. In particular, we don't know for sure if some of these processes can be extracted from a religious context and used in secular settings. Putnam and Lim's research suggests that this won't necessarily work. Their research shows that it is *religious* friends that matter, not friends in general.

## TAKING ADVANTAGE OF THE RELIGIOUSNESS-WELLBEING-HEALTH CONNECTION

It's not always necessary to understand exactly why a correlation exists to take advantage of it.

Back in the 18th century, observers began to note that when crew members ate fruit on sailing ships, it appeared to stop the devastating bane of scurvy. Slowly but surely, ship captains began to have their crews eat citrus fruits — including, for the British, lots of limes — and death rates dropped. Crew members were urged to eat fruit even without an understanding of exactly why eating certain fruits cured scurvy. Farmers in countries around the world figured out that putting bird, animal, and human waste on their fields produced much better crop yields — even if they hadn't the slightest idea why it worked. Smokers die sooner than nonsmokers, and life insurance companies act on this correlational knowledge in setting up their premium schedules — even if they don't fully understand the biological nature of the relationship. The people behind the famous FICO credit-scoring agency have observed all kinds of correlations between aspects of a person's financial behavior and creditworthiness. It is not necessary to understand what is behind these complex correlations to use them — which is exactly what the FICO people do when they assign you a credit score.

Similarly, I'm focused here on a pretty clear relationship between religiousness on the one hand and higher wellbeing and health on the other. Is there a way to take advantage of this knowledge even if we don't totally understand how it works?

This is not a trivial question, given the escalating cost of healthcare, massive outlays of federal tax dollars to pay for Medicare and Medicaid, and rapidly rising business insurance premiums. The religion-wellbeing-health connection has the potential to be of significant monetary importance.

It is quite possible that Americans will increasingly become aware of the potential benefits of being more religious in the years ahead (perhaps because of reading this book!). Americans may choose to become more religious as a way to increase their personal happiness and health. That could consequently lower healthcare costs for everyone.

Americans already use membership organizations to help reach wellbeing and health goals — including AA, Weight Watchers, local health clubs, and online support groups. Americans may decide to seek religion for these same reasons, choosing to be religious precisely because they are seeking practical outcomes. The choice to become religious — even if initially for practical reasons — could thus eventually lead to higher wellbeing as Americans attend religious services, develop and maintain social support networks within these religious settings, and adopt religion's explanations for life's setbacks and challenges and the promise of a better life ahead.

As I noted above, many religions forbid, either formally or informally, the types of behaviors that health and wellbeing plans focus on eradicating. These include smoking, excessive drinking, and self-indulgence. Americans seeking better health and wellbeing, in theory, have a penchant for eliminating these bad behaviors. Religion provides a way to help do this. So Americans may choose religion for these practical reasons.

Some churches already recognize the drawing power of an increased emphasis on the personal wellbeing benefits of religion. Large nondenominational churches feature support or covenant groups. Some have specific programs aimed at improving church members' fitness and health. The huge nondenominational Saddleback Church in California, as one example, has ventured directly into the health arena, promoting its "The Daniel Plan: God's Prescription for Your Health," which includes seminars with Pastor Rick Warren, Dr. Mehmet Oz, and other experts to talk about improving church members' fitness and health. In 2011, Warren himself lost a lot of weight and decided that he would use his church to help others do the same.

The Episcopal Health Ministries is also on the case, stating, "There is a significant need for the church to address health issues. The current health care system in the United States doesn't focus on health; it is primarily disease oriented. Too often it isn't a cohesive, holistic system; it's fragmented and enormously expensive. The church, on the other hand, is in the business of healing, of making whole, and of doing it in community. The local congregation is a place where health professionals and lay people can work together to keep people well, to empower and educate, to advocate for health and to care for people in need."

Gallup held a fascinating seminar on religion, wellbeing, and health in February 2012. One of the topics of conversation concerned the highly visible "New Atheism." Books by Richard Dawkins and Christopher Hitchens among others have received much visibility as they proclaim the virtues of atheism and the evils of religion. We members of the panel concluded that all of the research showing the benefits of religion has been hidden under a bushel. If this research does become more widely known, more and more people may well choose to take action as a result and become more religious.

Of course, we may be expecting too much with this prediction.

Many other clues to a healthier life are right in front of our faces, yet roundly ignored. Exercise, for one thing, is almost a magic potion for what ails most Americans. Generally, the more exercise we do, the healthier we are and will be — in part because exercise is correlated with losing weight. Eating vegetables and fruits in lieu of french fries, red meat, and sugar-laden drinks and desserts is also very healthy. Sleeping well, drinking only in moderation, and avoiding the irrational practice of inhaling harmful gases into the lungs also make us healthier. None of this is secret information. These paths to better health are widely known and widely disseminated. They are also widely ignored. Americans still take elevators, circle mall parking lots to avoid walking a few additional steps, and often strive to avoid exercise rather than embracing it. Consumption of bad foods is certainly not on a steep decline. More than one in five Americans still smoke. And many Americans are significantly overweight.

Knowing the path to health is clearly different from putting that knowledge into practice. But I think we are at a point of some convergence of a number of factors that will increase the chances that Americans will take action in regard to religion. One of these factors is the rapidly growing group of Americans who are entering their senior years, a group that will become more and more acutely aware of their physical wellbeing. Another is the increasing effort by businesses and government to try every mechanism possible to make Americans healthier — in the desperate scramble to control rising healthcare costs.

## THE POTENTIAL ROLE OF BUSINESS AND GOVERNMENT

Government and businesses want Americans to lose weight, exercise, stop smoking, and engage in other healthy behaviors. This is based on the proven connection between these changes and a lowered cost burden on the healthcare system. Indeed, businesses and insurance companies increasingly use incentive systems designed to reward activities related to less use of healthcare dollars — exercise, smoking cessation, and regular preventative health screenings.

Here's the controversial premise: *Religion* could be included in this list of behaviors. The basis for this would be an assumption that highly religious employees will cost a company less over time. Businesses could provide health insurance discounts to employees who demonstrate that they go to church — similar to the programs now in place for other healthy lifestyle practices like going to the gym. The idea would be to sustain religious involvement among those who are already religious or to foster an increase in religious involvement among those who are not religious. This would lead to healthier employees and not incidentally, lower an organization's overall health costs.

The Cleveland Clinic in Ohio stopped hiring smokers in 2007. The clinic also gives incentives for participation in exercise programs, gives big discounts for developing healthy living plans if the employee is overweight or has other signs of pending excessive use of healthcare dollars, and has banned unhealthy foods from its cafeterias. I don't believe that the Cleveland Clinic yet gives incentives to its employees who are highly religious. But this could in theory be just around the corner.

The federal government, including Congress and the executive branch, are now the prime movers in the attempt to lower overall healthcare costs. Of course, the government cannot constitutionally get involved in promoting any specific religion, even if for socially desirable reasons.

The federal government does, however, provide information to its citizens, which in turn they can use to make healthier decisions. The government has mandated that tobacco products carry large warning labels about the deleterious effects of using them; has spent a great deal of effort to require that food packages list ingredients and contents; promotes various easy-to-use representations of food groups and their place in a healthy diet; and under the aegis of its health branches, publishes an enormous amount of data about the health effects of various behaviors and lifestyle choices.

I remember the major emphasis that the Kennedy administration put on physical fitness, including promoting the 50-mile hike. First lady Michelle Obama more recently has become involved in a major effort to promote fitness and weight loss among the nation's young people. New York City Mayor Michael Bloomberg required chain restaurants in his city to carry dietary labels, and most recently, mandated a ban on the sale of large sodas in certain businesses in his city. The Affordable Care Act of 2010 included a big section focused on increasing the healthiness of Americans before they are ever exposed to the healthcare system. So in theory, the U.S. government certainly could include information about the proven connection between religiousness in general (not mentioning any specific religion) and wellbeing and health in its communication efforts.

All of this is highly controversial. Many people recoil at the idea of business and government encouraging *any* type of religion or dealing with religion in any way. Religion is a touchy subject. Still, I think the positive effects of religion are too strong and too universal to ignore, especially when billions of dollars are at stake. I believe there is the real potential that those with a big financial interest in the wellbeing and health of the nation's population are going to have to talk directly and deeply about religion.

## NATURALLY OCCURRING DEMOGRAPHIC PROCESSES

It's quite possible that religion will grow in influence in the U.S. in the years ahead as a direct result of an increased awareness of its positive effects on wellbeing and health. This trend will be helped along enormously by the inexorable forces of demographics.

The massive baby boom generation is now approaching the "golden age" of religion, the 65+ age range where religiousness peaks. As we will see in Chapter V, it's quite likely that aging baby boomers will become more and more religious, thus tilting the whole nation in a religious direction. In and of itself, this means we should have a healthier America because we have a more religious America. Baby boomers will also continue to look for ways to extend their health and maintain their wellbeing as they age.

We thus have before us a potential convergence. The next several decades may produce a boom in religion among the growing senior population in this country as a result of the fact that older people become more religious in general. And older baby boomers will quite possibly be hypersensitive to ways to improve their lives. All of this could produce positive outcomes for the nation's overburdened healthcare system.

---

### Bottom Line

Religion is correlated with positive outcomes in the U.S. today. Being religious is related to happiness, wellbeing, and health.

We don't fully understand how or why these relationships exist. But they are so commonly demonstrated and so powerful that I believe more and more people will pay attention to them in the future. If research continues to confirm a definitive religion-health connection, then the power of religion to help achieve some of the nation's most important social and fiscal goals — higher wellbeing and lowered healthcare costs — may be too significant to ignore.

Those entrusted with improving health outcomes and lowering healthcare costs may well end up having to focus on how to take advantage of the religion-health connection. Savvy health-conscious Americans may increasingly adopt religion as a mechanism to increase their overall emotional health, wellbeing, and physical health. Joining a church may become as common as joining a health club.

# CHAPTER IV

## Religion and Politics

The United States was founded on the premise of freedom of religion. The First Amendment declares: "Congress shall make no law respecting an establishment of religion, or prohibiting the free exercise thereof." John Kennedy referred to this constitutional mandate in addressing voter concerns about his Catholic religion in his 1960 election campaign. Fifty-two years later, Republican presidential candidate Rick Santorum said that Kennedy's affirmation of the separation of church and state almost made him "throw up" — because Santorum felt there *should be* a connection between religion and politics. Santorum did not need to worry. Despite the Constitution's formal prohibitions, the connection between religion and politics is alive and well in America today. Religion is heavily intertwined with the American political system.

Imagine that you have to guess whom a person on the street is going to vote for in the presidential election. You can ask only one or two questions. Asking a direct question about the projected vote or a political question of any sort is not allowed. I would ask, "What is your race?" If the person said he or she is white, I would ask, "How often do you go to church?" If the person responded,

"Weekly," I would predict that this person is highly likely to vote for the Republican candidate. If the person said that he or she seldom or never attended church, I would predict that this person is highly likely to vote for the Democratic candidate.

The final Gallup survey conducted before the 2008 presidential election showed a huge skew in voting by church attendance, with a 34-percentage-point swing in the margin of support for Barack Obama and John McCain between those who attended church weekly and those who seldom or never attended church. Gallup found the same patterns in the 2004 and 2000 elections. In 2004, there was a 26-point advantage for George W. Bush over John Kerry among those who attended church weekly. That compared with a 20-point advantage for Kerry among those who seldom or never attended church.

Gallup surveys indicated that Bill Clinton in both 1992 and 1996 did better than his opponent among those who seldom or never attended church. And our Gallup surveys in spring 2012 showed that very religious voters supported Romney over Obama by nearly 20 points, while nonreligious voters supported Obama over Romney by more than 30 points. It is a pretty well-established fact, in other words, that highly religious white Americans skew strongly toward the Republican candidate for president.

We have the intersection of two powerful forces in America: religion and the political sphere. The results have fascinating and important consequences.

## RELIGION AND POLITICS TOGETHER: STILL GOING STRONG

This is nothing new. Government and religion have been intertwined for as long as either has existed. Religious leaders have been political leaders. Political leaders have claimed to be divinely inspired religious leaders. Kings have adopted and used religion for their aims. Religions have been adapted to fit in with societies. The religion of Moses was intertwined with the rule of the pharaohs. Archbishop of Canterbury Thomas Becket was killed in England because of his views on the relationship between the church and the state. Ireland and Northern Ireland were split in large part because of religious differences between Protestants and Catholics. India and Pakistan were split in large part because of religious differences between Muslims and Hindus. Wars continue to rage around the world between groups defined by differing religions, and people continue to be attacked in the name of religion.

The United States has, as I noted above, a formal separation of church and state. No one church or organized religious group is directly or formally tied to government operations. Still, individuals' personal religious beliefs and their political behaviors and attitudes are highly connected. This relationship is far from trivial. It is a fundamental component of the U.S. political scene.

A couple of decades ago, Stuart Rothenberg and I wrote a book called *The Evangelical Voter* — building on the increasing interest in religion and politics at that time. A "born-again"

Southern Baptist, Jimmy Carter, ran for and was elected president in 1976. The president who followed Carter, Ronald Reagan, was not explicitly born-again nor a member of a fundamentalist faith, but he nevertheless built a coalition based in part on highly religious Republicans.

The focus on the interplay of religion and politics has intensified in recent years. George W. Bush was able to win his two presidential elections in significant part because his campaign team mobilized religious voters to support his re-election. In 2008, highly religious voters again supported the Republican candidate, John McCain, although Barack Obama's support was so strong overall that McCain lost.

In January 2012, a group of conservative religious leaders flew to Brenham, Texas, to meet at a Southern Baptist leader's ranch. Their mission? To deal with the possibility that Mitt Romney — a Mormon — was going to take the Republican Party's presidential nomination. These leaders talked, prayed, and took votes. They finally endorsed Catholic Rick Santorum as the best choice of those available — beating out another Catholic, Newt Gingrich; Protestant Ron Paul; and in particular, Mormon Mitt Romney. Of course, Santorum did not end up with the nomination. Eventually, most of these religious leaders did swing their support to Romney. But the key point here is how directly these *religious* leaders were concerned about what was happening in the *political* sphere.

Globally, the tragic events of Sept. 11, 2001, abruptly brought our attention to the power of religious beliefs to affect the secular and political world. Devout Muslims' religious beliefs lead to specific views on how the countries of which they are citizens should be run. Religion is at the interplay of much of what's happening in Egypt, the rest of the Middle East, and the Persian Gulf region. And religion intertwines itself in political disputes in Africa, Europe, and Asia.

In short, religion is a powerful factor in political and social issues in countries around the world and remains a potent force in American politics today — on the surface and quite strongly beneath it. I will not review the entire history of the relationship between religion and politics; that would take volumes. I'm interested in where things stand today. And on that front, there's a clear bottom line: *Religion and political status remain highly correlated in America today.*

"Political status" includes the political party with which one identifies as well as the candidate for whom one votes. Everything else being equal, the more religious an American, the more likely he or she is to vote for the most conservative political candidate available. Put in the context of party politics, we can say: *Everything else being equal, the more religious an American is, the more likely he or she is to identify as a Republican. The less religious an American is, the more likely he or she is to be an independent or a Democrat.*

This is my R and R rule: "Religion and Republicans." This remarkably robust finding persists across recent time periods, within groups, and in almost any context. I'll spend the rest of this chapter exploring what this means for the future of religion and politics in this country.

## R AND R: THE BASICS

The accompanying chart shows the "net" Democratic percentage — or the percentage identifying as Democrats in each group minus the percentage identifying as Republicans — by religiousness. The higher the bar, the more Democratic the group. Note that in 2009 and 2010, Americans overall ("All Americans") were more likely to identify as Democrats than as Republicans.

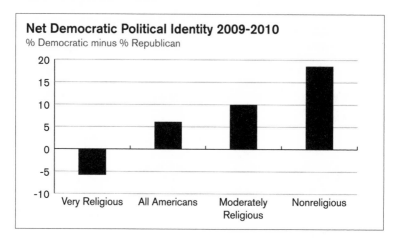

**Net Democratic Political Identity 2009-2010**
% Democratic minus % Republican

This is a pretty clear — and I would say remarkable — pattern. As Americans move across the spectrum of religiousness, from very religious to nonreligious, the bars get higher, signifying more Democratic identification. Very religious Americans' net Democratic score is about -6, which means that they were more Republican than Democratic (2009 to 2010) by a nearly six-point margin. Look at the nonreligious bar. These Americans are more Democratic than Republican by a margin of more than 18 points.

I compute religiousness using two variables: church attendance and self-reported importance of religion. The relationship between the first of these, church attendance, and party identification is detailed in the accompanying table.

**Political Party Identification by Church Attendance 2009-2010**

| | Republican | Independent/ Other/ Don't Know | Democrat |
|---|---|---|---|
| At least once a week | 36% | 32% | 29% |
| Almost every week | 32% | 32% | 33% |
| About once a month | 26% | 35% | 36% |
| Seldom | 24% | 38% | 36% |
| Never | 16% | 44% | 37% |
| Weekly church attendance minus never attend church (in percentage points) | +20 | -12 | -8 |

Church attendance appears to affect Republicanism most of all. *The drop in the percentage Republican across these five church attendance groups is as clear-cut as it gets.* Republican identification decreases from 36% among those who attend church at least once a week to 16% among those who never attend church. That is a drop of more than half.

The percentage of Americans who identify as Democrats, on the other hand, increases as church attendance decreases, albeit by not as much. This is in part because Democrats in the U.S. today include a significant number of black Americans — and blacks turn everything on its head because they are highly religious *and* highly likely to be Democrats. I have more to say about this paradox below.

The percentage of Americans who identify as independents increases significantly as church attendance decreases. This makes sense. People who are not attached to the system in a religious way (i.e., those who do not go to church) tend not to be attached to the system in other ways (i.e., they do not have a personal identification with a political party). *If an American does not attend church, he or she is more likely to be on the sidelines politically, more indifferent in political orientation, and less likely to be Republican.*

In short, you just are not going to find many Republicans among a randomly chosen group of Americans who never attend church. These religiously apathetic Americans are more likely to be politically apathetic — independents — than anything else, followed by identifying as Democrats. A group of Americans who attend church every week, on the other hand, are most likely to be Republicans and least likely to be Democrats.

This is a basic, stable phenomenon in American politics today — similar to the finding that women are more Democratic than men. And this phenomenon persists even as political tides roil America's partisan makeup.

I analyzed Gallup data collected between 2009 and 2011. This was a time during which Americans became more Democratic as Barack Obama took office as president, and then became less Democratic as the bad economy dragged on in 2010 and 2011. But these broad trends in party identification did not disrupt the differences caused by religion. The very religious remained most likely to be Republican, and the nonreligious remained most likely to be Democrat.

More recently, I computed the 2012 presidential election vote choice based on self-reported church attendance — from interviewing Gallup conducted in April and May 2012. For reasons I will get into below, I looked just at non-Hispanic whites — by far the largest voting group in American politics. The results were startling. Romney beat Obama by 46 points among those who attend religious services weekly, while Romney lost to Obama by 22 points among those who never attend religious services.

Democratic leaders reading this may be asking, "Are we missing something here?" The Democratic Party appears to be leaving many highly motivated, emotionally connected religious Americans to seek their political identity elsewhere.

## R AND R RULE PERSISTS ACROSS RELIGIOUS GROUPS

American Jews (along with Muslims) are the most Democratic religious groups in America today. Mormons are the most Republican. There are certainly Republican Jews — I think of Sammy Davis Jr., who was black, Jewish, and supported Richard Nixon. There are also a few Democratic Mormons (Senate Majority Leader Harry Reid comes to mind). But these are relatively rare examples.

Protestants — the largest religious group in America — tilt slightly Republican. Those who identify with non-Christian religions, those with no religious identity, and to a degree Catholics are more likely to identify as Democrats.

But, and this is a keenly important point, regardless of your brand of religion, if you are highly religious *within* that brand, you are more likely to be Republican than if you are an apathetic practitioner of that brand. In other words, *our R and R rule persists across almost all religious groups in America today.*

Highly religious Protestants are more Republican than less religious Protestants. Highly religious (i.e., more Orthodox) Jews are more likely to skew Republican than less Orthodox Jews. Highly religious Catholics skew more Republican. Even the small group of people with no religious identity who go to church are more Republican than those who do not.

## Evangelicals

Jimmy Carter, a born-again Southern Baptist, was and still is very public about his religious beliefs. He was of course the governor of Georgia who ran for and won the presidency in 1976 — becoming one of the nation's few Baptist presidents. From that point on, the labels "evangelical," "fundamentalist," and "born-again" became an increasingly important part of the social and political fabric in our society.

Just who are these evangelicals? Well, that's an easier question to ask than it is to answer. The book I wrote with Stuart Rothenberg, *The Evangelical Voter,* focused on just this question back in the 1980s. Everybody, it seemed, was interested in this newly defined group of more activist Protestants who were energized to take political action on behalf of their religion. Nobody agreed on how to define them.

Some researchers just ask respondents in surveys, "Are you an evangelical (or born-again)?" For example, Edison Research, which runs the exit polls in election years, asks voters fairly simply if they define themselves as evangelical or born-again Christians. Other researchers get very technical. The Barna Group uses a series of nine questions — including belief in the literalness of the Bible, having had a born-again experience, and so forth — to isolate "true" evangelicals.

I do things a little differently. I start by excluding Catholics because they are different enough to warrant special study. I then isolate highly religious non-Catholic Christians, thus ending up with a group of *highly religious Protestants* — basically the functional equivalent of evangelicals. This group is much more heavily Republican than less religious Protestants.

The accompanying chart shows net Democratic identity by church attendance among Protestants. The lower the net Democratic identity, the higher the net Republican identity.

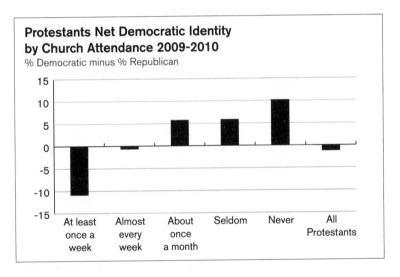

**Protestants Net Democratic Identity by Church Attendance 2009-2010**
% Democratic minus % Republican

Notice the difference in political identity between those who attend church at least once a week and those who attend church almost every week. This distinction between attending services *at least* once a week and *almost* every week seems minor. But is very discriminating. Those who attend church at least weekly — remember, these are Protestants — constitute an exceedingly Republican group. These core, very religious Protestants represent the group most people have in mind when they talk about evangelicals.

Among those who attend church *almost* every week, it is a rough tie between Republican and Democratic identification. As church attendance drops below that point, so does Republican identification. Protestants who never attend church are the most Democratic of all Protestants.

These data are for *all* American Protestants. That includes a healthy proportion of blacks because the vast majority of blacks in America today are Protestants. Blacks are a fascinating group of Americans from a political and religious perspective. Their political and religious identities are predictable and fixed. Blacks are the most religious *and* the most Democratic race or ethnic group in America. I'll return to this important group below.

Many definitions of evangelicals are based only on *white* highly religious non-Catholic Christians. These white *Protestants who attend church regularly are skewed even more strongly toward the Republican Party and away from the Democratic Party, by about a 5-2 ratio.* This is a nice summary of one of the most important political realities in American society today and one that should be copied in bold into every politician's playbook: **Highly religious white Protestants constitute a powerful political group in contemporary politics, and this group is strongly Republican in its political orientation.**

## Roman Catholics

Two major Republican presidential candidates in the early spring of 2012 were Catholic — Rick Santorum and Newt Gingrich. Mitt Romney's vice presidential candidate in 2012 was Catholic. This might convince a naïve observer that Catholics are a major factor in today's Republican Party. The naïve observer would be wrong.

Catholics as a whole skew more Democratic and independent than do Protestants. But, and this is the interesting part, the religiousness of a Catholic *does* affect his or her political orientation — predictably.

Very religious Catholics are considerably less Democratic in orientation than are nonreligious or lapsed Catholics. The net Democratic advantage among Catholics who are very religious is +4. It rises to +13 among those who are not religious. So it is not too surprising that Republicans Santorum and Gingrich are very religious Catholics.

This difference within the Catholic population is stronger among white, non-Hispanic Catholics, the very religious of whom are more Republican than less religious Catholics, as we would predict. Religiousness does not add as much to understanding the political orientation of *Hispanic* Catholics — although it still makes a slight difference.

## Jews

Jewish religious leaders in the U.S. have to live with the fact that they get a low "yield" from their constituents on a week-in and week-out basis. Synagogues just are not consistently very full. About 65% of Jews report that they seldom or never attend religious services, making them one of the least religious groups in America.

This lack of active religious participation fits with the fact that American Jews are also very Democratic, one of the most Democratic subgroups in the American population today. Still, among that small group of devout Jews we would categorize as very religious — a lot of whom we assume are Orthodox — we find the predictable tendency for a more Republican political orientation.

This tendency is not so great that it overwhelms the strong Jewish Democratic orientation that is a dominant feature of American politics. But highly religious Jews are clearly more Republican and less Democratic than Jews who attend services less frequently. This gives us additional confirmation of our R and R rule.

## No Religious Identity

Americans who have no explicit religious identity are very unlikely to be Republican — with a net Democratic over Republican political identity of +25.

At the same time, there are *some* Americans with no religious identity who are still very religious, based on their self-reports of going to church and saying that religion is important in their daily lives. And these people are more Republican and less Democratic than all the others of their "no religious identity" ilk. This again reinforces the power of our R and R rule: *To be religious is to be Republican.*

## R AND R RULE PERSISTS ACROSS AGE AND GENDER

Stop a 20-year-old in America on the street today. If this young person is very religious, he or she is more likely to be Republican than a 20-year-old who is nonreligious. Then stop an 80-year-old. Lo and behold, you find exactly the same pattern. A very religious 80-year-old is more likely to be Republican than a nonreligious 80-year-old.

This is another truly remarkable affirmation of the power of what appears to be the near-universal religion and politics connection. *From the youngest American adult to the oldest, those who are more religious are significantly more likely to be Republican.*

We get the same results regardless of gender. *For American men **and** women, those who are highly religious are the least Democratic, those who are moderately religious are more Democratic, and those who are nonreligious are the most Democratic of all.*

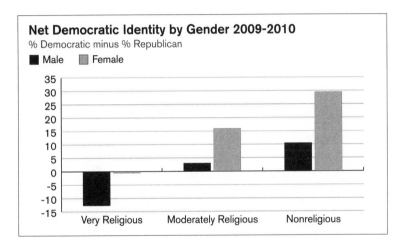

**Net Democratic Identity by Gender 2009-2010**
% Democratic minus % Republican
■ Male  ▨ Female

This is not to say that gender doesn't matter in politics. It does. Women in America *are* more likely than men to be Democrats — the famous gender gap you hear a lot about. But women are also more likely to be religious than men. This creates a fundamental paradox. As we would say statistically, there is an *independent* effect of gender on political orientation, and there is a separate *independent* effect of religiousness on political orientation. They both have an effect.

This a paradox because these relationships seem contradictory. Women in this country today are inclined to be Democratic in their political orientation, everything else being equal. At the same time, women in this country are inclined to be more religious, which predicts that women should therefore be more *Republican*, according to our R and R rule. If you are a woman, then please understand that you are thus subject to cross-pressures. *There is a cultural pattern pushing you to be more Democratic. There is also a cultural or genetic pattern pushing you to be more religious.* These two pushes are in generally contradictory directions.

Yet, and this is my point here, these two "pushes" don't cancel each other out. Even though women as a whole tilt Democratic, the more religious the woman, the more Republican she is — just as is the case with men.

## THE R AND R RULE AND ETHNICITY/RACE

### Hispanics

Hispanics in America today skew Democratic and independent. They are less likely than the average American to be Republican. The overall net Democratic advantage among Hispanics is higher than +20. Republican political candidates still believe that Hispanics are a swing group of sorts and in the 2012 political campaign, actively courted them, although spring 2012 data showed that Hispanics preferred Obama over Romney by about a 2-to-1 margin.

Still, our R and R rule — religion leads to Republicanism — holds. There are slightly more Republicans and fewer Democrats among Hispanics who are very religious than among those who are not religious.

This is a more subdued pattern than we found for whites, among whom identification with the Republican Party essentially falls off a cliff as religiousness drops. This same pattern among Hispanics, by contrast, is modest. Still, the tendencies are in the predicted direction.

## Asians

Any ethnic group "other than white" in America today skews Democratic in political orientation. Certainly, this holds true for Asians, who are significantly more likely than whites to identify as Democrats or independents, regardless of church attendance. But, within the context of this reality, our R and R rule again raises its head. *Asians who are religious are significantly more likely to identify as Republican than those who are nonreligious.*

## Blacks

Supreme Court Justice Clarence Thomas and former presidential candidate Herman Cain are two unusual Americans. Both men are black and Republican, not a typical combination. There are just not a lot of Americans who possess these two characteristics simultaneously.

Based on our overall R and R rule, people who share racial and religious characteristics with Thomas and Cain should be very common. Black Americans, after all, are the most religious racial or ethnic group in this country. Therefore, they should be the most Republican group in this country. But they are not. Blacks are overwhelmingly Democrats. They confound our basic R and R rule. Expectations are turned on their head when it comes to blacks in the U.S.

Blacks are not so religious just because they overwhelmingly tend to be Protestant — one of the most religious groups in the country. Black Protestants are more religious than white Protestants. Blacks' high level of religiousness is also not generational. Americans of all races become more religious as they age. By the time Gallup first interviews young black men and women — at ages 18 to 29 — they are already more likely to be religious than are 18- to 29-year-olds of other race and ethnic groups. And blacks consistently retain a higher level of religiousness up through the oldest group of those aged 65 and older. The higher level of religiousness for blacks does not appear to be a vestige of older patterns that are slowly fading away as the population ages. In similar fashion, gender does not seem to matter. Black men are more likely to be very religious than are non-black men. Black women are more religious than non-black women.

## Why Are Blacks More Religious?

The historical, cultural, and normative patterns that developed in the black community in its early years in the U.S. all contributed to higher levels of religiousness today. Blacks were brought to the U.S. as slaves and held in slavery for several centuries. It is widely assumed that black slaves developed religion as a defense mechanism against their inhumane daily living circumstances and potentially hopeless existence. The promise embodied in the religious tradition of the South is hope ahead beyond this earthly pale. This religious tradition emphasizes a relief from the earthly sorrows imposed in this lifetime.

Of course, critics have noted that those in positions of power had a lot of incentive to encourage black slaves to be religious. Slave owners knew that religion would help calm the slaves and help discourage rebellion. As one historian put it, "Large slaveholders ...

worked to comprise a Christian primer for slaves to instill teachings that were designed as a response to the portents of revolution, and to serve as preventive measures to any insurrection."

There is also the simple fact that blacks in past centuries and to this day disproportionately live in the South, the most religious region of the country. Thus, blacks are strongly meshed into a culture of religious intensity. Had blacks been brought to this country as slaves in Northern states, or had blacks immediately immigrated to other regions of the country as freed men and women, it is doubtful that they would have ended up being as religious as they are today.

There were still other reasons why blacks became religious centuries ago. Black slaves were not generally allowed to read books (for those who were literate). But the Bible was okayed by many plantation owners — presumably in part for the reasons I mentioned above, that owners may have thought religion would help dampen revolutionary fomenting among blacks.

Churches were one of the few edifices that blacks were allowed to build and use exclusively in plantation days. This helped foster the church as the central organizing fulcrum for black culture. Again, owners encouraged black churches because they welcomed the influence of religion among their slaves. Even after the Civil War, the church may have remained the one community gathering place that was "safe," helping instill the church as a major component of blacks' lives.

Blacks may also have related to the situation of the Israelites in the Old Testament because the Israelites were eventually released from bondage. Blacks may have found comfort and inspiration in the fact that the man they believed to be God's son, Jesus, was similarly reviled in his life; God's beloved was a lot like them.

## The Paradox

Regardless of the original causes, it is clear that the black community in the United States continues to carry with it a strong normative culture of religiousness. The black community in the United States also carries with it a strong Democratic orientation. These two facts create the central paradox of blacks' relationship to religion and politics in America today:

- Blacks are substantially more religious than the average non-black American.

- Blacks are much more likely to be Democrats than the average non-black American. In fact, some *70% of blacks in 2009 and 2010 identified as Democrats.* That compares with 33% of all Americans. *Only 5%* of blacks are Republicans. That compares with 27% of all Americans in 2009 and 2010.

This creates a fascinating "strange bedfellows" situation. Our R and R rule predicts that religion leads to Republicanism. That most certainly has not been the case when it comes to black Americans. Women in America are cross-pressured between their higher levels of religion on the one hand and their tilt toward the Democratic Party on the other. Now we are talking about a similar, but more substantial, cross-pressured situation among blacks in the U.S.

*American blacks are generally either Democrats or independents. Very few blacks, regardless of their religiousness, identify as Republican.*

*Republicans have no foothold of strength among blacks, regardless of their religious intensity.* And that's that. The same factors that cause religious non-black Americans to affiliate with the Republican Party seem to break down when it comes to black Americans.

Just as there are historical reasons that explain why blacks are so religious, there are historical reasons that explain why blacks are so likely to be Democrats. The Democratic Party has long adopted positions that were in sync with the interests of blacks, embracing policies oriented toward blacks as far back as Franklin Roosevelt's first election in 1932. Harry Truman, a Democratic president, helped desegregate the armed forces after World War II. John F. Kennedy, another Democratic president, came to the aid of black civil rights protesters in the South during his administration. Democratic President Lyndon Johnson pushed for the passage of the milestone Civil Rights Act of 1964.

Since LBJ, most Democratic presidential candidates and most other major Democratic candidates at the federal and state levels have continued to court and count on overwhelming black support. Almost all black representatives and black senators are Democrats. Barack Obama, the first black president in U.S. history, is a Democrat. There is probably no stronger link, bond, or connection in American politics today than the one between being black, identifying with the Democratic Party, and voting for Democratic candidates.

Republican leaders give lip service to their efforts to attract more black voters. But most realize that it is a losing cause. *Blacks in America, despite their high level of religiousness, remain steadfast in their loyalty to the Democratic Party and do not — as is the case with other religious Americans — skew politically toward the Republicans.*

## Culturally, Blacks Should Be Republicans

In the fall of 2008, it became apparent that blacks in California were not following the lead of their fellow Democrats in opposing Proposition 8, a proposed law that defined marriage as only between a man and a woman. Blacks in California, by all available evidence, supported the proposition in line with other religious voters. One exit poll estimated that only 36% of Democrats voted in favor of the proposition, compared with 70% of blacks. In the same poll, 82% of Republicans voted in favor. Thus, blacks were just 12 points away from the Republican vote on Proposition 8, but they were 34 points away from the Democratic vote.

This result on California's Proposition 8 vote is not unique. On a number of social issues, blacks' attitudes diverge from those of their fellow Democrats. The reasons for this are fairly clear. Blacks are more religious than the average Democrat, which in turn makes them culturally different. Blacks' religiousness affects their positions on social issues — creating big cross-pressures. Blacks strongly identify with the Democratic Party. Because they are religious, blacks' values and cultural orientations skew toward those of Republicans.

Overall, black Americans are at least somewhat more conservative than Democrats on same-sex marriage, divorce, gambling, stem cell research, sex between an unmarried man and woman, having a baby outside of marriage, gay or lesbian relations, doctor-assisted suicide, abortion, cloning animals, and suicide.

Barack Obama has publicly announced that he supports legalized same-sex marriage. Gallup data show that while 46% of Americans and 60% of Democrats interviewed from 2008-2012 support this position, 39% of blacks agree. Given Obama's strong influence in the black community, perhaps attitudes will change in the years ahead. But for now, blacks' position on this hot-button issue is closer to that of Republicans — among whom 24% support legalized same-sex marriage — than to that of Democrats.

I don't see any evidence yet that the religion-politics paradox among blacks is going to change in the years ahead. Remember that young blacks today appear to be as disproportionately religious as their parents and grandparents. There is also no evidence that American blacks will abandon the Democratic Party in the years ahead and increasingly become Republican, regardless of moral and values positions. It looks like the paradox will endure.

## WILL DEMOCRATS FIND RELIGION?

Much of what we have looked at in this chapter brings us back to our basic R and R rule: *Religious intensity is correlated with Republican political identity in the United States today.* It's not a perfect relationship. There are atheistic Republicans out there, just as there are highly religious Democrats. But the GOP and ideological conservatism have clearly become the home for highly religious white Protestants. This relationship between religiousness and politics persists across age groups and among men and women. To be religious is to be Republican.

Deeply religious Americans have in recent years shown the most concern about issues with a connection to procreation and the family — abortion and same-sex marriage being the most prominent. Religious voters see the GOP as the party most aligned with their beliefs on these issues. The GOP has shrewdly welcomed them with open arms.

The connection between Americans' religiousness and their political party orientation is, in other words, a two-way street. Deeply religious people have decided that the Republican Party provides the best political mechanism for ensuring that their religious beliefs are represented in the political sphere. GOP leaders for their part have sensed the tremendous value in the energy and emotions of deeply religious voters. GOP leaders made the decision to grab hold of, activate, and take advantage of these sentiments. The Republican Party has, over the years, assiduously courted highly religious voters.

We certainly saw the embracing of this connection in the 2012 campaign for the Republican presidential nomination. Mitt Romney was a moderate governor of a traditionally liberal state (Massachusetts). But at the national level, highly religious Republican voters are more conservative than moderate and favor laws that restrict abortion, same-sex marriage, and stem cell research. Highly religious Republican primary voters did not initially see Romney as the best candidate to promote these issues. Rick Santorum in particular hurt Romney by positioning himself as the family values candidate. Santorum won the votes of highly religious Republicans in a number of southern states in the process. Romney had to work hard to convince these religious Republicans that he was the appropriate recipient of their political loyalty.

Democrats traditionally have not courted religious voters. The result has been the increasing tendency for the Democratic Party to be the home for moderately religious and nonreligious white voters.

This could change. In February 2012, I was surprised to see that President Barack Obama and his advisors were beginning to rethink this traditional positioning (and without the benefit of having read this book!). At the National Prayer Breakfast in Washington, D.C., Obama took on the relationship between politics and religion more directly, at great length, including his statement: "In my moments of prayer, I'm reminded that faith and values play an enormous role in motivating us to solve some of our most urgent problems, in keeping us going when we suffer setbacks, and opening our minds and our hearts to the needs of others."

Obama's explicit recognition of the connection between religion and politics was very unusual for a Democrat, most of whom have generally stayed clear of any association between religion and politics. But in this speech, Obama directly invoked religion as a justification for his political philosophies, convictions, and actions. This represented a clear expansion of the religion-politics connection the likes of which we have not seen historically from Democrats.

Basically, Obama was implying that Jesus would have been a Democrat. That's quite an assertion. But Obama implicitly makes the case that a deeply religious follower of Jesus would, on the issues he lists, be more in line with traditional Democratic positioning than with Republican positioning. Of course, ever ecumenical, Obama also peppered his speech with references to the Islamic and Jewish religions.

Obama did not in his speech take on the family values issues on which Republicans have traditionally focused. He instead pivoted his view of the role of religion toward a focus on broad economic, social justice issues: financial institutions playing by the same rules as everyone else; insurance companies not discriminating; unscrupulous lenders not taking advantage of the poor; sympathy for seniors, young people, and the middle class who have financial problems; preventing atrocities and human trafficking; caring for the poor; and giving everyone a fair shot. As Obama said, "We can't leave our values at the door."

This reminded me of "liberation theology," the idea that the religious teachings of the New Testament imply the liberation of the poor and suffering from their dire situations. Shannon Craigo-Snell, a theologian at Louisville (Kentucky) Presbyterian Theological Seminary, explained to *The New York Times* in May 2012: "Liberation theology, at its most simple, is the Sunday school Jesus who healed the sick or took care of the poor people. It's what your Sunday school teacher taught you if you grew up in a church. It isn't something people should be afraid of, unless they're invested in poor people not getting fed or sick people not getting healed."

Obama's speech stood out because Democratic candidates have historically made the de facto case that religion is a private, personal affair. Democrats don't like to talk about religion. Obama upended that historical norm.

It's possible that other Democrats will follow Obama's cues in the years ahead and argue as he did that religious convictions should lead to more *liberal* positions on a number of issues. This might not have a high probability of converting large numbers of religious whites to the Democratic Party. But it would be a start.

Highly religious white Americans are a valuable political target. The default now is for these religious white voters to skew Republican. When Democrats ignore religious voters, it is thus tantamount to ceding the majority of them to the GOP.

Religious voters are valuable for reasons beyond their sheer numbers. Religious voters are often easily mobilized through radio, television, Internet sites, religious publications, churches, and other religious organizations. This mobilization in turn leads to high voter turnout, sustained campaign support, and financial contributions. Plus, highly religious Americans are by definition passionate about their beliefs. This passion is easily channeled into emotional fervor and intense support for political candidates.

Large numbers of highly religious white Christians are not going to become Democrats or vote for Democratic presidential candidates any time soon. The Republican-religion connection is well-ingrained. Deeply religious Americans are often fundamentalist in their beliefs, not only on biblical and moral issues, but also in their politics.

But, as Obama and his advisors obviously are beginning to figure out, Democrats could certainly *try* to shift this ingrained connection. It doesn't take a lot of movement to change the outcome of close elections. Deeply religious independents who lean Republican are in theory up for grabs. More than one-third of white independents, for example, attend church weekly or almost every week. About three out of 10 white independents consider themselves to be born-again or evangelicals. The majority of these evangelical voters tilt toward the GOP. But they, and perhaps other "loose Republicans," could be open to persuasion if the Democrats can figure out how to reach them.

It may be a Democratic candidate's willingness to *engage in the debate* on the proper role of religion in government policy that matters most. The key in many religious voters' minds is the use of the political arena as a mechanism for bringing about moral change. The most significant downside of the current Democratic approach is its failure to acknowledge this connection. Democrats have been missing in action on this front. Religious voters looking for candidates who address head-on the question of the role of government relating to issues of morality and ethics in American culture thus turn to Republicans.

Democrats in theory would benefit from having positions on the issue of religion and politics — *any* positions — than simply to sidestep the matter altogether. Even Democratic candidates who believe strongly that there should be no direct connection between religious foundational beliefs and policy could make their rationale for this position explicit and clear.

There is little doubt that highly religious white voters have helped the Republicans win elections. Democrats need to decide if they want to ratchet up their competition for this valuable bloc of voters. Obama's speech is a possible beginning point. It may signal an increased inclination for Democrats to develop more specific positions on the relationship between personal religious beliefs and the political realm. In the process, Democrats would thus reach out to those who sincerely believe that religious beliefs and convictions should be a guiding force in public policy on selected moral issues.

## *Bottom Line*

I think highly religious Americans will increasingly be identified in the future as very fruitful, important targets for political mobilization. *Potential* religious energy converted to *kinetic* religious energy is — or can be — extremely powerful. Republicans are well aware of this. Democrats have been less so. If Democratic leaders continue to ignore highly religious Americans, their party will increasingly miss one of the nation's most important voting blocs in the years to come.

# CHAPTER V

## Age and Religion: The Fascinating Relationship

We may witness a major increase in religiousness in the U.S. in the next several decades because of demographic shifts in the American population. Churches will boom; religious literature will dominate bestseller lists; and religious programs will become mainstays on radio, television, and the Internet.

The explanation for this lies in the inevitability of changes in the nation's age structure. Older Americans are more religious than younger Americans. The inexorable aging of the huge baby boom generation will swell the ranks of older Americans. If baby boomers follow the pattern of their elders, we will have ever-increasing ranks of the religious in the U.S. for years to come.

At least that's the theory. And this theory carries with it a giant assumption. The assumption is that baby boomers will become more religious as they age, just like those who came before them. My review of the data suggests this is likely — but by no means a certainty.

At the same time, there may be countervailing forces. There is the possibility of a decrease in religiousness if younger Americans decide in increasing numbers not to get married and if the U.S. birth rate continues to decline.

All of these potential shifts in the culture of religion in America revolve around the most fundamental demographic variable in any society — age. Social scientists love age as a variable because it is so objective and predictable, unlike many of the squishy attitudinal variables we study. A person's age each year for the rest of his or her life is fixed. Almost all survey respondents know their age, and most accurately report it to survey researchers. And the number of people at any particular age in the future is highly knowable just by making projections based on the number of people at various ages now.

Religion in America today is highly related to age. The possibility of changes in the nature of this relationship, changes in the relative size of the age cohorts that make up the population, and shifts in the two key demographic patterns of marriage and childbirth all lead to the potential for significant shifts in the religious landscape in the years ahead.

## AMERICANS GET MORE RELIGIOUS AS THEY GET OLDER

The fact that older Americans are more religious than younger Americans most likely comes as no great shock. Those venturing into neighborhood places of worship will be hard-pressed not to notice the gray hair, bald heads, and stooped posture of many of those sitting therein. Those venturing into the vicinity of colleges or youthful neighborhoods on Sunday morning are not very likely to be trampled by large hordes of young people moving en masse to their nearest church or other place of worship.

There are exceptions, of course. There *are* very religious young people. Youthful quarterback Tim Tebow is quite religious and quite public about it. His pointing to heaven and adopting the "Tebow" prayer stance after a winning play has become a cultural phenomenon. Earlier in his career at Florida, Tebow inscribed Bible verses on the black sunblock under his eyes. Young basketball sensation Jeremy Lin is also highly religious and public about his evangelical Christianity.

And, of course, there are older people who are quite *nonreligious*. One of the most famous of the "New Atheists," British biologist and *The God Delusion* author, Richard Dawkins, is in his 70s. Christopher Hitchens, explicit atheist and author of the book *God Is Not Great*, was 62 when he died in 2011.

But these exceptions notwithstanding, it is fundamentally clear that age and religiousness rise together. Religious worship attendance and self-reported importance of religion are higher among Americans in their 40s than those in their early 20s and more dominant among those in their 70s than those in their 40s.

This age-religion relationship is not confined to the U.S. Princeton economist Angus Deaton examined Gallup World Poll data from around the world. He found that old people are more religious than young people in all but 16 of the 142 countries he looked at. The exceptions — that is, countries where younger people were more religious than older people — included Israel, two sub-Saharan African countries, and Georgia.

Gallup interviewed more than 700,000 Americans in 2009 and 2010. We asked every one of these people their age. We then asked them if religion is important in their daily lives and how often they attend worship services. This gives Gallup, as far as I know, the biggest sample sizes ever available for any researcher investigating religion. This is important because we get no data on religion from the U.S. Census Bureau or any other government agency. And most private surveys asking about religion include only 1,000 to 2,000 interviews.

The accompanying graph displays most of what you need to know about the basic relationship between religiousness and age. Each line represents one of our three religiousness groups. I determined these groups by combining religious importance and church attendance. The height of the lines shows the relative percentage of Americans who are in each religiousness group at each age point.

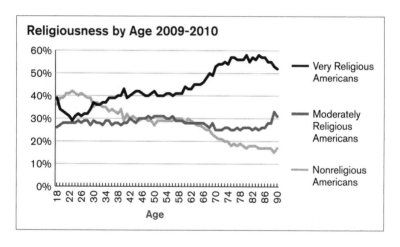

My tweet about this graph would be: "Americans get more religious as they age. Knowing a person's age thus significantly increases our accuracy in predicting his or her religiousness." (That's more than 140 characters, but I'm going to let it stand.)

The statistical *correlation* between age and being very religious for these data is 0.94. That's an amazingly high number, given that the highest correlation possible is 1.0. Again, simply knowing a person's age is an excellent predictor of how religious he or she is.

Are you 23 years old? If so, too bad from a religious perspective. You are at the least religious age point of your adult life. Are you 80 years old? Well, if so, you are at the exact opposite end of the religious spectrum from 23-year-olds; 80-year-olds are the most religious Americans. More than three times as many 80-year-olds are very religious as nonreligious. You are highly likely to see 80-year-olds in church on Sunday morning. Any 23-year-old you spot in church is a rare find.

The age-religion connection is not precisely linear. Americans' religiousness rises as they age, then levels off, and then rises again.

- Eighteen-year-olds start out being fairly religious. This is likely because many of the 18-year-olds Gallup interviews are still living in their parents' home. Religiosity drops off rapidly after age 18 as young people leave their parents' home. Leave the home, leave the church. Religiousness bottoms out at age 23.

- Americans show a fairly steady upswing in religiousness from age 24 to about age 40. This represents the period of time when young people traditionally settle down, get married, and have children. Religiousness essentially levels off as Americans get into their 40s.

- Then come the baby boomers. Religiousness across the roughly 18 years of the baby boom generation — those aged 48 to 66 in 2012 — pretty much continues to just sit there. The youngest baby boomers, born in 1964, are essentially no more likely to attend church than baby boomers born 15 years earlier. We do begin to see an increase in religiousness in the oldest baby boomers — those now in their 60s.

- Americans' religiousness begins to rise fairly steadily from their early 60s until they are in their late 80s. After that point, religiousness drops off, primarily because these older Americans are less able to attend religious services.

This gives us four major age-related phases of Americans' religiousness today:

1. **The low point**, when Americans are in their early 20s.

2. **Growth stage I** begins when Americans reach their mid-20s and ends in their early 40s.

3. **The plateau stage**, when Americans are in their 40s and 50s.

4. **The resurgent growth stage II** begins when Americans are in their 60s.

## GROWTH SPURT IN RELIGIOUSNESS

Age 23 is the Death Valley of American religious topography — the lowest point across the entire adult life span. From age 24 on, to continue the topographical analogy, we witness a steady upward climb until Americans reach their 40s — a move from

Death Valley, to, let's say, the top of Humphrey's Peak in Arizona — not the highest point in the land (that's reserved for the Mount McKinley of old age) but decidedly higher than where Americans start in their early 20s.

Why do Americans become more religious as they age from 23 to 45?

Remember our starting point: Very young adults — those aged 20 to 23 — are the *least religious* Americans of all. The reasons for that are not hard to fathom. Think back to when you were in your early 20s — freed from the bonds of family structure; most likely on your own for the first time in your life; probably very mobile, moving from place to place; and no doubt experimenting with the freedoms that come from being out in the world as an official adult. All of this can lead to a reduced focus on religion.

When Americans reach their mid-20s, we begin to witness a bounce back from this veritable abyss of irreligion into which young people sink as they leave their homes in their late teens. Some of this religious renaissance could be biological — that is, an evolutionary "kicking in" of a mental interest in religion and the spiritual realm that grows with age. It is also most likely associated with life changes. People in their mid-20s gradually pull back from the late adolescent/early adulthood phase in life in which they rebel and experiment. By age 25, young adults typically are more settled, have begun careers, and in general have an increased involvement in all aspects of their community — including church. Becoming more religious could also reflect a growing interest in the meaning of life.

Two other things happen with remarkable frequency in young adults' lives during these years: Americans get married, and

Americans have children. *Both of these occur simultaneously with an increase in religiousness.* Very few Americans are married at age 20. By age 40, about 80% of Americans are married or have been married. Very few Americans have children at age 20. Within 15 years, three-quarters of Americans have a child in the home.

## Exploring the Marriage Factor

Ask a 42-year-old American on the street, and there is a 66% chance that he or she is married, plus a 14% chance that he or she is divorced or separated — in other words, previously married at some point. As a result, that 42-year-old has less than a 20% chance of never having been married — a big difference from a 20-year-old, whose chance of never having been married is more than 90%. Young Americans are also becoming more religious as they age from 20 to 42, as we have seen. It seems reasonable to ask if these two trends are related.

On a person-to-person basis, marital status *is* related to religiousness. Married 18- to 42-year-olds are the most religious of all, followed by those who are separated, then by those who are divorced, and then by those who are single/never married. The least religious of all are those who are living with a domestic partner.

Still, as I discussed in Chapter III, correlation is no proof of causation. The fact that two things vary together — in this case, the marriage rate and the religiousness rate in the young American population — does not necessarily mean that one causes the other. Correlational relationships are quite often complex and difficult to figure out. (Drinking coffee is correlated with the sun rising. One of these does not cause the other, however. Being a Harvard graduate is correlated with success. Because Harvard admits only people demonstrated to be highly motivated, smart, and in most cases already successful, it is not clear that a Harvard education per se has anything to do with Harvard graduates' later success. And so on.)

Several things could be happening here. Let's look at what the data show about each of three possible scenarios:

- **Scenario 1: Americans get married as they age through their 20s and 30s, and the results of being married could cause these young people to become more religious.** This does not seem to be borne out directly by the data. Religiousness increases across Americans' 20s and 30s *regardless* of whether they are married. Americans who are *not* married are more religious in their late 30s and early 40s than in their early and late 20s. This means that the tendency for Americans to get more religious as they age through their 20s and 30s is generally independent of marriage.

- **Scenario 2: Americans become more religious as they age through their 20s and 30s, and the results of being religious could cause these young people to want to get married.** This too is not strongly supported by the data. Nonreligious Americans get married as they age, just like the very religious. This means that the "urge to marry" through this age span is independent of religion. Something else is at work. The forces that push young people to get married (social, economic, cultural, genetic, etc.) operate on all Americans no matter how religious they may or may not be. Indeed, multivariate statistical analysis shows an independent effect of age on religiousness even when marriage is controlled for.

- **Scenario 3: Marriage and religion could have nothing to do with one another. The simple process of getting older could cause young people to get married and independently cause them to become more religious.** This explanation seems to fit the data best. Age by itself appears to be the big factor. As Americans age through their 20s and 30s, a couple of things happen: They are more likely to be religious, and they are more likely to get married. The data suggest that these two things occur together but do not necessarily cause one another. The data clearly show that Americans are likely to get married as they age regardless of their religiousness. Americans also get more religious as they age regardless of their marital status.

It's important to note at this point that fewer young people today are responding to the urge to marry. Change is afoot. The marriage rate is dropping among young people in the U.S. Those who are getting married are doing so later in life.

These changes are fairly dramatic. As the Population Reference Bureau (PRB) stated: "Marriage rates have dropped precipitously among young adults ages 25 to 34 during the past decade and the decline has accelerated since the onset of the recession, according to PRB's analysis of new data from the U.S. Census Bureau's 2009

American Community Survey (ACS) and 2010 Current Population Survey (CPS). The data suggest that more young couples are delaying marriage or foregoing matrimony altogether, likely as an adaptive response to the economic downturn and decline in the housing market."

Look at these trends in the Gallup data. The percentage of 18- to 42-year-olds in our sample who are married has dropped from 47% in 2008 to 40% in 2011.

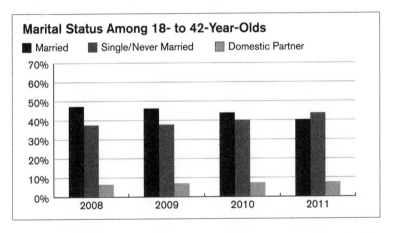

As demographic changes go, that is pretty dramatic. Exactly why young people are becoming less likely to get married is not entirely clear. Some people who study such things think it is because of the economy, as the Population Reference Bureau researchers I quoted above seem to believe. Young people seemingly do not want to commit in an uncertain economy. Perhaps they do not want to spend the money to get married. Being less likely to afford a house may also affect the desire to get married. More general uncertainty and anxiety might make it easier for young people to live together and not formalize their relationship. Marriage implies a stable future, which young people may not be sensing today.

For our purposes, the reason for the drop in marriage rates is not as important as its possible effect. My conclusion is that getting married *does not* appear to be the major reason why people become more religious. This means, of course, that a decrease in the marriage rate shouldn't affect the religiousness of young people. In fact, that is exactly what we find. We do not see signs — at least to date — that the drop in marriage rates is causing Americans to become less religious. The percentage of 18- to 42-year-old Americans who can be classified as "very religious" has stayed generally constant since 2008, with only a slight indication of a drop in religiousness in 2011.

*This is an important finding.* We know that fewer young Americans are deciding to get married these days. This may be a temporary phenomenon that will turn around as the economy gets better. Whatever the future of marriage, however, it does not look like it will dramatically affect religion. We do not see a significant decline in religiousness rates among younger Americans despite the fact that these individuals are getting married at a less frequent rate. Young Americans are becoming more religious as they age through their 20s and 30s — just as their older brothers and sisters and their parents did before them.

## Having Children

Now, let's turn to the other relentlessly regular event that occurs as young Americans age. They have children.

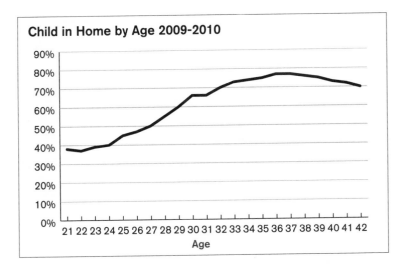

The shape of the curve in the accompanying chart does not come as a great surprise, certainly. Biology has dictated that childbearing is generally confined to women's teens, 20s, and 30s. Cultural norms have reinforced this natural state of affairs. Thus, we find that by the time Americans reach age 37, 77% have a child in the home. That compares with 37% of Americans at age 22 who have a child in the home. As we know, Americans also increasingly become religious from about age 22 to age 40 or so. Thus, just to summarize, as Americans move through the ages 22 to 40:

1. They increasingly tend to have children.

2. They increasingly become more religious.

Therefore, it is reasonable to assume that having a child causes one to become more religious. Let's see if the data support that.

- Americans with children become more religious as they age. Americans aged 40 to 44 who have children are more religious than Americans aged 25 to 29 who have children.

- But, Americans without children do *not* tend to get more religious as they age into their 40s; the relationship between age and religiousness among those without a child is relatively flat.

Thus, it seems that having a child opens Americans up to becoming more religious in their 20s and 30s. If Americans were banned from having children at age 18, everything else being equal, they would probably not be nearly as likely to become more religious as they age through their 20s and 30s. *Having children does appear to affect one's desire or impulse to be religious.*

We can ponder why this is the case. Having children may activate parents' maternal and paternal instincts, and those could include an attraction to religion. Having children may activate feelings that lead to awareness of one's mortality, of the goodness of life, of one's responsibility across many spectrums of life, and of one's responsibilities in a broader sense, all of which in turn may lead to religion. The miracle of birth itself could activate religious awe. Having children also may represent a more practical feeling that it is time to settle down — a marker, as it were, for entry into a new phase in life. With that new phase could realistically come an increase in religious interest.

Parents certainly worry about their kids' education, socialization, and learning. This concern could extend to religion. Regardless of whether parents themselves are actively involved in church and religious activities, they may feel the need to expose their kids to religion.

Parents may also see a benefit from having their children learn the moral standards and education that typically come with religious socialization. Parents may feel there are practical considerations of the benefits of church attendance for little ones, exposing children to other young kids and helping them learn to interact socially. In the process of exposing their children to religion, parents — even if by accident — can become more involved in religion and church themselves. (Church leaders, being no fools, realize all of this of course and often use programs for children as a way to market to parents.)

There is another possibility. Being religious could cause people to want to have children. In other words, while having a child could make parents more religious, it's possible that religious people could be the most likely to want to have children.

We don't have to look far for examples. Mormons actively encourage their members to have many children, backed up by complex theological justifications. The Catholic church still discourages artificial birth control, which in turn encourages childbearing. Young people of all faiths who are intensely religious may generally be more inclined to focus on family and cultural aspects of life, which could include children.

However, the data don't show a big drop in religiousness among 18- to 42-year-olds in recent years, and we *do* see a drop in fertility. So this "reverse causality" explanation doesn't appear to be highly plausible, although it certainly could be a factor in all of this.

When it comes to having children, the times, they are a changin' — just as was the case with marriage. Americans are having fewer babies. The nation's fertility rate peaked in 2007 and has been significantly lower in the years since. Gallup data show that the percentage of 18- to 42-year-olds with children in the home has been dropping slightly over the last few years: from 61.8% in 2008 to 61.5% in 2009 to 60.4% in 2010 to 58.1% in 2011.

This isn't a huge change, but fertility does appear to be slowing down. If having children leads to increased religiousness, then we could see at least slightly lower religiousness levels in the population in the years ahead. We do not see this yet. We see no significant change in religiousness among 18- to 42-year-olds in recent years. But if the drop in fertility accelerates, changes could begin to show up.

As was the case with the drop in marriage rates, one can assume that the economy is a big cause of the drop in fertility in the United States. Economically depressed young people without jobs and with pessimism about the future may simply conclude that it's not the right time to have children. If the economy improves, the fertility rate could get back on track — with its presumed religious consequences.

## The Ethnic Composition of the Younger Population

Hispanics will almost certainly be an increasing percentage of the younger U.S. population in the years ahead. This is a result of the large number of young Hispanic immigrants to this country in past decades. These immigrants had many babies. These children are now growing up and thus keeping the percentage of Hispanics in the population growing. This foretells a continuing increase in the Hispanic percentage of the population. And, because Hispanics are more religious than non-Hispanics, this means a more religious general population.

I should note that Hispanics are less likely to be married and more likely to be in domestic partnerships than non-Hispanics. But, the data show that Hispanics living in domestic partnerships are more religious than non-Hispanic domestic partners. In other words, being in a domestic partnership does not seem to lead to the same decrease in religiousness among Hispanics as it does among non-Hispanics.

Overall, it looks like the increase of young Hispanics as a proportion of the U.S. population helps predict an increase in the nation's average religiousness in the years ahead.

## THE BABY BOOM THUNDERS INTO OLD AGE

Millions of American World War II soldiers and sailors came home to get married and start families after the war ended in September 1945. The result? The baby boom, an unprecedentedly large group of babies who were born into these post-World War II families. The baby boom generation's sheer numbers have and will continue to affect American society in many ways. I am a card-carrying member of this generation, if you consider a driver's license to be a card.

We baby boomers have now started moving into retirement age. As has long been predicted, this is beginning to affect the government programs designed to help seniors: Medicare and Social Security. These two programs are going to be overloaded in decades to come as huge numbers of baby boomers are added to their rolls. But, we baby boomers are going to have a big effect on a lot more than just these two entitlement programs. One thing we are going to affect is religion.

About 38% of the 18+ U.S. population was between the ages of 45 and 64 in 2009-2012, which roughly defines the baby boom. Only 17% of Americans were between the ages of 65 and 84. Over the next 20 years, baby boomers will be 65 to 84 years of age. This means the population in the 65- to 84-year age group could double in the next 20 years. Of course, some baby boomers will not make it over the next 20 years. Even with normal attrition, however, the 65+ age group is going to be a lot bigger in 20 years than it is today.

This age shift is important to religion because — as we have seen — Americans' religiousness begins to increase rapidly at about age 60. Taken as a whole, net religiousness (percentage very religious minus percentage not religious) for today's baby boomers is +12; net religiousness for those 65 and older is +32.

The big picture? Two things are going to happen in the next several decades. First, most of our country's very religious seniors are going to die. They will take their high level of religiousness with them to the grave. Second, they will be replaced by baby boomers who, as of today, are much less religious.

Now, here is the very important fork in the road: If baby boomers keep the same relatively low level of religiousness they have now as they age, then older America is going to be a lot less religious than it is now. Because the size of older America is going to roughly double, this would lower the average religiousness of the entire U.S. population.

On the other hand, what if baby boomers become more religious as they age, adopting the religiousness of their fathers and mothers? In that case, the current group of seniors will be replaced by a much larger group with the same high level of religiousness. This means that average religiousness in the country will go up because we will have so many more religious seniors.

## UNDERSTANDING WHY SENIORS ARE MORE RELIGIOUS IS CRITICAL TO UNDERSTANDING THE FUTURE

It's easy to take for granted the fact that older Americans are more religious than younger Americans. We see the gray hair and stooped posture of those in the pews on Sunday. We observe the older age of popes and heads of various religious bodies. We tend to assume that this is just the way it is. But it's worth looking at possible explanations for this phenomenon — explanations that might help predict what is going to happen in the future as the current crop of old people is replaced by a new crop of aging baby boomers.

**1. Older people are closer to death, and they increasingly confront illness and frailty. Religion is a way of coping with these inevitabilities.** I hear this explanation for the age-religion connection most often. People become more conscious of the pending arrival of the grim reaper as they move through their 60s, 70s, and 80s. The older they get, the closer they are to death, and the more they see death around them. Older individuals also tend to increasingly have health problems, which lead to concerns about dying. Thoughts about mortality raise the *Alfie*-esque question "What's it all about?" Religion can provide answers to that question.

Plus, older Americans are mostly retired, and the main body of their work and child rearing is behind them. Older Americans thus have more free time to ponder mortality and the meaning of life.

All of this presumed worry about death and concern about what happens after death logically and inevitably — the theory goes — brings with it an increased embrace of religion. Most religions, by design, help assuage the pain of death and offer promise of life after we die. Ministers, priests, rabbis, and chaplains are typically called in when a person is seriously ill or on death's doorstep. It is not an accident that the immediate aftermath of death is typically a religiously oriented funeral service. Turning to religion seems to be a very natural part of the aging process.

The idea that religiousness increases when one faces death is a part of our folklore — "There are no atheists in foxholes." In the current setting, the argument is "There are no atheists in retirement homes." We are old, we see death, we become more religious.

I remember watching the funeral services of Elizabeth Edwards, the estranged wife of former presidential candidate John Edwards. Elizabeth had been diagnosed with cancer six years before she died and knew she was dying. In the nationally televised funeral service, Elizabeth's minister talked about visiting her in her final days. He reported asking Elizabeth if she had "accepted Jesus Christ as her personal savior," and he reported that she had emphatically said "yes." Preparing for her death religiously was a significant concern as she approached death.

What happened to passengers of US Airways flight 1549 that made the extraordinary landing in the middle of the Hudson River on January 15, 2009? As the powerless plane descended toward the water, its passengers were confronted with the stark reality of the possibility of death. And for many, what happened was a quick, dramatic turn to religion. News accounts from passenger interviews after the landing included memories of "passengers quietly praying, some reciting the Lord's Prayer, others asking for God's help." From the self-described "not overly religious" to the devout, many of that plane's passengers turned to religion and prayer as they faced the possibility of dying. As one passenger said, "I knew I was in God's hands."

I don't know if any of these passengers had been reading *The God Delusion* before takeoff on that ill-fated flight. I wonder what Richard Dawkins would have been doing if he were on that plane. Certainly not, according to his own words, praying to a God he is at militant pains to argue does not exist.

Turning 70 or 80 is not quite as dramatic as being told by your pilot that your plane is about to crash in the middle of the Hudson River. In theory, however, it could have the same effect on religiousness.

If seniors become more religious in an effort to maintain positivity in the face of negative life events such as dying and getting sick, it seems to be working. *Older Americans are actually emotionally better off by most measures than those who are younger.*

Additionally, seniors actually seem to worry less about death than those who are younger. Gallup and other pollsters do not routinely ask Americans how often they worry about the meaning of life, death, and so on. But, in 1990, Gallup did ask Americans the simple question "Do you fear death, or not?" The answers showed that 23% said "yes." But this self-reported fear of death actually *declined* rather than increased with age. A third of those aged 18 to 29 said they feared death. That dropped to 25% among those aged 30 to 49 and to only 16% among those aged 50 and older. A separate question in that poll asked respondents how often they thought about death. Just 16% said "very" or "somewhat" often. And that percentage was 15% among those who were older.

So, the data show that older Americans worry about death less, worry less in general, and have the highest wellbeing. These data could reflect the fact that religion *is* doing its work well — warding off the fear, pain, and angst of death in Americans' older years. Evidence does suggest that religion actually helps cause higher wellbeing, as we saw in Chapter III. It is certainly possible that the need for higher wellbeing in the pending face of death and illness causes people to adopt religion, which in turn produces higher wellbeing as intended. Our data show, in fact, that very religious senior citizens (those 65 and older) report having a better life "today" than those who are less religious, and they anticipate having a better life in the future.

About 31%-32% of Americans who are between their 60s and their early 70s have health problems. The incidence of health problems begins to rise slowly after that point, as Americans move into their 80s.

Does worry and concern over these health issues lead seniors to be more religious? That's a tricky question to answer. Americans in their 60s with health problems *are* very slightly more likely to say that religion is important to them in their daily lives than those who report they don't have health problems. But this is not a major distinction. And by the time Americans reach their 70s, there is no difference in importance of religion between those who do and do not have health problems. Gallup also measures Americans' self-reported incidence of "physical pain." There is a slight tendency for older Americans with pain to be more likely to say religion is important in their daily lives, particularly those in their 60s. This is, however, a modest relationship. It helps explain only a little of the overall tendency for religious importance to increase as people age.

Again, these are not major, dramatic relationships. Overall, *seniors who have pain and who have health problems are generally a little more likely to be religious than those who don't.* But because the relationships are not large, it gives us pause as we ponder the theory that older Americans are more religious because they seek solace for their health problems.

**2. The number of widows and widowers increases with age, as does the percentage of women in the senior population — and those who have lost a spouse and women have above-average religiousness.** The accompanying graphic is pretty depressing to married Americans now entering their 60s and 70s. It shows how quickly married Americans become widows and widowers, particularly after age 70. By the time Americans are in the 85- to 89-year range, only about 30% remain married — less than half of those who are married at age 55. This reflects the fact that the percentage of Americans who lose a spouse expands year by year from age 60 on.

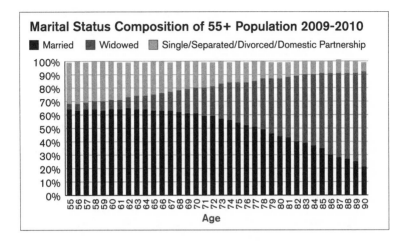

Those who have lost a spouse are more likely to say religion is important and to attend church than those who are married. We can ponder the reasons why. The most obvious explanations are those I mentioned previously: Losing a spouse causes one to be reminded how close death is and/or to be grieving and lonely. The hypothesis is that these — and other factors — are responsible for driving widows and widowers back to church and to religion.

This expansion of widows and widowers as a percentage of the population could explain part of the general uptick in religiousness between ages 60 and 90. This is analogous to what happens in the 25- to 49-year age range when single people are replaced by married people. In Americans' older years, married people are in turn replaced by widows and widowers — and although married people are more religious than singles, widows and widowers are in turn more religious than those who are married.

But this explanation has its limits. I have looked carefully at the data. They show that those who have lost a spouse *and* those who are married get more religious as they age into their early 70s.

Age seems to be working its religious magic regardless of marital status. Americans certainly become more likely to be widows and widowers as they move through their 60s and 70s. But the overall jump in religiousness is *not* just a result of the increase in widowhood. If, hypothetically, all older people remained married all their lives and both married partners died on the same day in all cases, there would still be an increase in religiousness as they age. If one-half of all married Americans lost their spouses at age 65, there would still be a steady increase in religious importance as these widows and widowers got older.

Here's some more depressing news for us baby boomer men: If things continue as they are now, we are going to die off a lot quicker than baby boomer women.

Slightly more than half of 60- to 64-year-olds are women, a number that rises to more than 60% among those aged 85 to 89. This is the result of the unfortunate fact that men die earlier than women. We know that women are demonstrably more religious than men, which I will explore in detail in Chapter VII. Some of the increase in religiousness could be, in theory, because of the representation of more women in the population as it ages.

But my analysis shows this is only a small part of the equation. The overall increase in the importance of religion rises almost as fast when we weight the data to be equal for men and women throughout this age spectrum as it does for "real world," unweighted data. There is no evidence that the higher death rate among men is a major causal factor behind the rising religiousness of older Americans.

**3. Older Americans are more religious because they grew up in more religious times and have kept their high levels**

**of religiousness ever since.** This explanation says that older Americans' higher levels of religion have nothing to do with being old and everything to do with the fact that they were socialized and inculcated into religion when they were young. This is a seemingly plausible explanation for the fact that seniors are more religious. I'll have a lot more to say about this idea in the next section.

Other explanations for the age-religion connection include the simple idea that older Americans are wiser and more open to the benefits or reality of religion. Or that older Americans have more time on their hands and therefore are better able to get involved in the aspects of organized religion and going to church.

## AS THE BABY BOOM AGES

Whatever the cause, the fact remains that as of today, those aged 65 and older are the most religious segment in American society. The much less religious baby boom generation sits there waiting its turn to be the nation's seniors in the years ahead. What is going to happen as this demographic transformation takes place? The answer will have a profound effect on the religious landscape in America.

The facts are clear. The older segment of the population is set to explode in size in the years ahead as the huge baby boom generation gets older. Baby boomers have affected everything around them all their lives. They are going to continue to do so as they get older.

Baby boomers will almost certainly become bigger users of the healthcare system as they age. Because there are so many baby boomers, this means the healthcare system in this country will have to enlarge. That is going to occur no matter how much baby boomers monitor their health and do everything possible to remain healthy. The Medicare system set up by the government to provide healthcare to senior citizens will expand. So will Social Security. Ultimately, sad to say, baby boomers will cause a boom in the use of the nation's funeral homes. Both the healthcare system and the business of helping families in their time of final need will be growth industries.

Travel and vacation services will grow as baby boomers scratch their travel itch in retirement. There may well be an increase in interest in pets, golf, and volunteer activities. Politics is going to be affected, as will popular culture. If baby boomers take a fancy to gardening or cooking, these industries too will boom.

For our purposes, the question is whether there will also be a "boom" in church pew manufacturers, religious publishing companies, and financial organizations that issue church bonds — all potential beneficiaries if aging baby boomers get more religious.

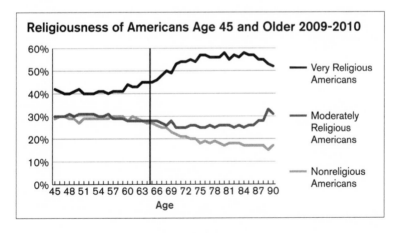

Baby boomers — those to the left of the vertical line in the graph — are much less religious than those in their late 60s, 70s, and

80s. As we have seen, two things can happen as this huge group of baby boomers gets older in the decades ahead:

- **Scenario A:** Baby boomers will *not* get more religious as they age. Religion in America will thus be in big trouble as highly religious older Americans die off and are replaced by huge numbers of less religious baby boomers.

- **Scenario B:** Baby boomers *will* become more religious as they age and will begin to take on the high level of religiousness of their mothers and fathers. Because there are so many baby boomers, religion in America will thus boom, creating a veritable golden age of the sacred.

Scenario B requires a giant leap of faith, so to speak. But I think this leap of faith is warranted. It is a good bet that we are going to see a religious renaissance among baby boomers as they age. *As a result — and as long as younger Americans don't stray from religion in huge numbers — the country as a whole will become substantially more religious in the decades ahead.*

## Two Explanations

Television advertisers covet programs that deliver big numbers of younger viewers. That's why so much television and cable programming is aimed at the young, leaving older viewers to watch old movies and Lawrence Welk reruns. Advertisers like young viewers, it is said, because of differences in receptivity to television commercials across the age spectrum. Young people are supposedly open to experimentation and trying new products and services. Older people are purportedly set in their ways and are much less affected by advertising blandishments. There is, in other words, a big age difference in how people relate to television advertisements.

This is but one example of thousands of cognitive and attitudinal differences between old and young people. Another is politics. Senior citizens are more likely to be Republican than those under 30 and also much more likely to vote. Senior citizens are less likely to favor the legalization of marijuana and less supportive of gay marriage. Lots of people have spent lots of time studying the causes of these types of differences in age groups in society. In the broadest sense, the results frequently devolve into two ways of explaining why people are so different at various age points. These explanations have a lot to say about the future of religion in this country.

First, there is the *generational* explanation for age differences. This explanation assumes that what happens as we age is fairly fixed. What happened to your grandmother when she became 65 will happen to you when you become 65 and will happen to your children when they become 65. Thus, the generational approach assumes that *each* generation becomes more religious as it ages. Baby boomers will automatically become more religious as they age through their 60s, 70s, and 80s, just as the generations that came before them did.

Second, there is the *cohort* explanation that focuses on the uniqueness of every generation — a uniqueness that results from the specific experiences that affected people in different age groups as they grew up. If this is the case, it's too late for baby boomers to change. Baby boomers' religiousness was set in stone as they grew up; they will keep their current lower levels of religiosity with them until they die. The gray and balding pates we currently see in church will gradually become relics of the past. Baby boomers will be out attempting to re-create the halcyon days of their youth as they age, not sitting in churches.

If the generational explanation is right, America as a whole will become more religious because the bulk of the baby boomers will become more religious. If the cohort explanation is right, we will see nothing but emptier and emptier pews in the future.

This is an example of a fascinating and important focus in the study of demography. People are what they are for many different reasons. I today reflect the influence of my upbringing in Texas, my parents, my peers, and the social forces that were at play as I developed through adolescence and early adulthood. I also reflect the fact that at my age, I'm subject to a bunch of "standard" forces that have affected and will affect everyone who is about my age. How these balance out is a key to the future of religion.

A cohort is simply a group of people we follow from their early to late years of life. Sometimes, a cohort's circumstances early in life are so significant and so unusual that they influence those in the cohort for the rest of their lives. This is a Freudian approach to religion, assuming that our early, formative years stay with us and affect us until we die.

Tom Brokaw bestowed the name the "Greatest Generation" on today's seniors. Americans in their 70s, 80s, and 90s were indelibly affected not only by the Depression but by the tumultuous years of World War II. The presumption is that these and other events forever shaped the Greatest Generation's outlook on life.

Many of today's seniors are Depression babies. They learned early on what it's like to have no money and no food, if not directly, then because of what they saw around them. Many also remember (or participated in) World War II and its associated traumas. All of this has led to an indelible Depression mentality — a part of this cohort's lifelong state of mind. These Depression babies were frugal in their 20s and continue to be frugal in their 80s. From a cohort explanation viewpoint, this frugalness among today's senior citizens resulted from the particular set of one-time-only circumstances that occurred when they were growing up. Members of the next generation may not be nearly as frugal as they move into their older years because they did not live through the Depression. Each particular cohort of people, in other words, is different and will remain different throughout its life course — not because of some inevitable process of aging, but because of their particular life experiences.

We baby boomers did not experience the Depression or World War II. But we did grow up in some pretty unusual circumstances. I don't remember any major negative economic forces that hung over my early years as I grew up. The 1950s and 1960s were generally booming, as I recall. The interstate highway system was built, we sent a man to the moon, cities were rapidly expanding, and jobs were plentiful. The economy was growing and expanding, and I think I believed it always would. The future looked unlimited. Everyone assumed they would do better than their parents did.

At the same time, not everything was perfect. We older baby boomers went through a lot of turmoil in the 1960s and 1970s. We are the Vietnam/Woodstock generation, raised in a time when rebellion was in the air, fostered in large part because of an unpopular war, the draft, and upheavals in race relations in this country. We lived through Flower Power, hippies, the Beatles, Kent State, riots, and long hair.

Many older baby boomers were particularly affected by the Vietnam War, which was a major factor in the thinking and consciousness of my generation, mainly because young men of my age cohort faced the draft and the possibility of going to war. Much of the hippiedom, rebellion, and "live for today" mentality that reigned in the late 1960s and early 1970s probably resulted from these war pressures.

Even 40 years later, baby boomers today may be rebellious, suspicious of authority, and less dogmatic than our fathers and mothers. Baby boomers developed a special sense of our own brand identity. We have been told all our lives that there are a lot of us, and we consider ourselves special.

You see where I am going with this. A cohort perspective on religion assumes that older Americans today are more religious than younger generations because of the circumstances in which they grew up. As members of this older group die off, they will take their high religiosity with them. The baby boomers who follow will bring *their* particular set of early life circumstances with them as they age. If the baby boom is indelibly stamped with its particular generation's characteristics, then their ways of thinking and feeling are not going to change.

That's one way of looking at it. The other is the generational explanation, which focuses more on life stages that affect everyone — no matter when they were born. Regardless of their cohort, people certainly act, think, and feel the way they do at least in part because of their age. The same generational forces replicate themselves across decades and even centuries.

The best way to look at this is to think about physical changes. When you think "generational," think "inevitable." Men 60 and older on average have less hair (and that hair is grayer) than men aged 18 to 29. This pattern would have been found in a cross section of men 100 years ago. Most probably, barring medical advances and cosmetic techniques, it will be found among a cross section of men 100 years from now. As people move through middle age, they have a harder time reading small print. More than 200 years ago, Benjamin Franklin observed the same pattern, and he invented bifocals to deal with it. Again, barring medical advances, we would expect to find the same age difference in ability to read fine print 100 years from now.

As humans age, other things happen — most of them bad. Older people get wrinkles in their faces just like they did in the olden days and as they will in the future (again, barring technological breakthroughs). As they age, people increasingly have heart problems, their bones shrink (many actually get shorter), they lose bladder control, their memory fails them, and their hearing becomes less acute. These age-related facts of life are relatively constant across time. They are not, for the most part, dependent on anything specific about any particular group of people in any particular generation.

All in all, a generational approach to the aging baby boom assumes that baby boomers will be subject to the same forces that affected their parents. As far as religion is concerned, this means baby boomers will become more religious just as their parents did.

At this point, baby boomers are not as religious as those aged 65 and older. If baby boomers' lower levels of religiousness are imprinted into their consciousness by the events of their earlier years, then we might assume this isn't going to change. That in turn would mean the replacement of religiously "fixed" older Americans with a new cohort of religiously "less fixed" Americans. But, if baby boomers' religiousness is *not* fixed, then the baby boomers *will* gradually become more religious as they age — affected by the same forces that affected their parents.

## THE EVIDENCE POINTS TO A GENERATIONAL APPROACH

The evidence I see supports the generational explanation more than the cohort explanation. *Age differences in religious consciousness existed years ago. They exist today. And they probably will exist in the future. This phenomenon doesn't appear to be specific to one particular generation.*

I have looked at a good deal of Gallup (and other) data. Overall, religiousness generally appears to drift upward with age regardless of the time period when the data were collected. Older people were more religious than younger people in the 1960s and 1970s. Older people are more religious than younger people today.

Back in the mid-1960s, Gallup data showed that 34% of 21- to 29-year-olds attended church. That compared with 44% of those 70 and older. In the mid-1970s, the difference in church attendance between these two age groups was 16 points. And as we have seen, these same types of differences in church attendance persist today. We find the same patterns in the comprehensive NORC General Social Survey data. Across all recent decades extending back to the 1970s, church attendance increased with age.

In other words, at least for the last 45 years or so, age differences in church attendance have been the norm in the United States. This pattern persists regardless of the particular time in history when the data were collected. These age differences in church attendance do not appear to be a function of idiosyncratic cohorts, but rather a function of recurring generational patterns that occur across decades.

## BABY BOOMERS ARE BECOMING MORE RELIGIOUS RIGHT ON SCHEDULE

Religiousness was beginning to increase among Americans who were at the older edge of the baby boom in 2010 and 2011, based on an analysis of the huge Gallup Daily tracking database. This is a key finding worth looking into in more detail.

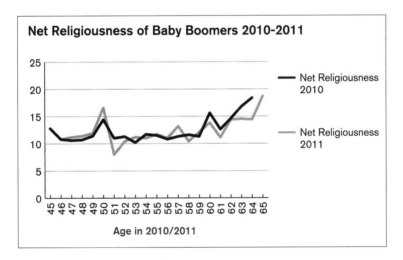

Baby boomers are *already* beginning to get at least a little more religious as they begin to enter their mid-60s. The most religious baby boomers, as we would expect, are those who were age 64 in 2010 and age 65 in 2011.

The oldest baby boomers are getting more religious despite the fact that the overall population is not getting more religious. Non-baby boomers were no more religious in 2011 than they were in 2008. Clearly, baby boomers are behaving as expected, getting more religious as they move into their 60s.

This chart shows church attendance for those aged 61 to 64 from 2008 to 2010. These highly detailed data give us a wonderful opportunity to see what is going on with the leading edge of the baby boomers as they enter their early 60s.

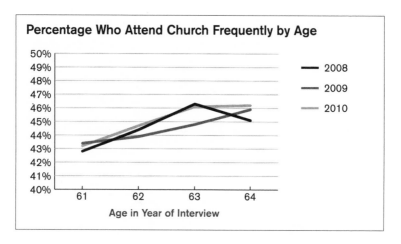

Frequent church attendance increased marginally across each age group from age 61 to 64 in data collected in 2008, in 2009, and in 2010. More importantly, my analysis suggests that those born in 1946 (the oldest baby boomers) attended church more frequently each year as they aged from 61 to 64. These "1946s" were more likely to be attending church in 2010 than they were in 2009 and more likely in 2009 than they were in 2008.

The differences are not huge, but they reflect the pattern we would predict based on a generational approach to aging and religiousness. If this pattern continues, average church attendance for those born in 1946 will climb again in the years ahead as they reach their late 60s and move into their 70s. And we assume the same thing will happen as those born in 1947, 1948, 1949, 1950, and so on move through their 60s.

All in all, the high level of religiousness among older Americans appears to be a permanent fixture of society. It is likely that baby boomers will become more religious as they age, just like those they are replacing. Americans in their mid-60s, the leading edge of the baby boom, are already getting more religious as we would expect if the generational hypothesis is the correct explanation for the age-religion relationship. *All of this suggests the possibility of a major increase in the average religiousness of the American population in the years to come as more and more baby boomers cross the 60-year-old barrier.*

There are many more baby boomers in the population today than there are seniors. The bulge in the population between about age 48 and 66 in 2012 will become a bulge between ages 68 and 86 in 20 years. If this population bulge carries high levels of religion with it, as I think is likely, the nation as a whole will become increasingly religious.

---

## Bottom Line

The future of religion in the U.S. depends in part on what happens to Americans who are now at very specific age points. We expect younger Americans to continue to get more religious as they age through their 20s and 30s, even though the data show that fewer Americans are getting married at this stage of their lives. The drop in the rate of having children could have an effect on young Americans' religiousness, but so far, this effect appears to be minimal.

The available evidence suggests that baby boomers will most likely get more religious as they age, for the same types of reasons that cause those now in their late 60s, 70s, and 80s to be religious. This will increase the overall religiousness of the U.S. population in the decades ahead.

# CHAPTER VI

## State Cultures of Religion: Why Mississippi Is Vastly Different From Vermont

A sociological observer from a distant planet would get quite a different picture of religion in the United States depending on where he (it?) happened to set down his spacecraft.

Landing in Vermont, the sociologist would find a group of people who tended to slough off religion altogether. He would observe relatively few residents venturing out on Sunday morning to engage in group ritual worship behavior.

Landing in Mississippi, however, the sociologist would find a highly religious culture. He would observe large numbers of residents leaving their houses on Sunday morning to worship — well over half on most Sundays.

Traveling to Alabama or Louisiana or Utah, the sociologist would find frequent group ritual worship patterns very similar to what he found in Mississippi.

Landing in Oregon or Alaska, the sociologist would observe patterns quite similar to what he found in Vermont: relatively few people attending church, many professing no religious beliefs.

What's going on here, the observer would ask?

We know that states differ significantly in the "brand" of religions that are most prevalent in each. Mormons predominate in Utah, Catholics in Rhode Island, and Protestants in Mississippi. The number of residents with no religious identity is way above average in Vermont and Oregon. Each religious group gets a different "yield" from its adherents. The high religious yield among Mormons is a major explanation for Utah's higher religiousness relative to other states. However, the high concentration of more religious Protestants in the South and the prevalence of residents with no religious identity in Vermont do not completely explain those states' highly different religiousness — as we will learn presently.

Highly religious southern states also have a high percentage of black residents. Blacks are the most religious racial or ethnic group in the U.S. That in theory could help explain why southern states are so religious. But it doesn't help explain why Maryland, which also has a high percentage of black residents, is not so religious.

In fact, the religious composition of a state, the racial composition of a state, and other demographic differences across states are but part of the story. Taking the Protestants out of Mississippi still leaves us a highly religious state. Taking those with no religious identity out of Vermont still leaves us with a very nonreligious state. Taking blacks out of the South still leaves a highly religious South. And Rhode Island is pretty nonreligious whether we take out or leave in that state's Catholics.

Our visitor from outer space would conclude that there is something fascinating and unique going on in the United States. The individual states appear to have differing "state cultures," which are themselves associated with higher or lower levels of religiousness. Every state in the country, from the one with the largest population (California) to the one with the smallest population (Wyoming) includes highly religious *and* nonreligious residents. But the states differ quite substantially in terms of the average religiousness of their residents. I think one good explanation for these differences in average religiousness is each state's *culture*.

The idea that states have different cultures certainly is not a surprise to presidential candidates. These candidates essentially ignore the majority of the 50 states each presidential election year. Why? Because cultural voting patterns in most states are so well-established that their residents are going to vote one way or the other regardless of the candidates who happen to be running.

Residents in "red" states such as Utah, Wyoming, Idaho, and Alaska are conservative and reliable Republican voters year in and year out. There is not going to be much campaigning by either presidential candidate in these states, which in all but landslide years will go for the Republican candidate. Residents in "blue" states such as Rhode Island, Massachusetts, and Hawaii are much less conservative and are reliable Democratic voters. Presidential candidates are not going to bother with them either.

These state cultures clearly relate to religion just as much as they relate to politics. Residents of New England and some of the "newer" states of the West are, for a variety of reasons, the type of people who have low levels of interest in religion. It appears likely that when new residents venture into these states, they are acculturated into these less religious normative patterns.

On the other hand, the South has within its boundaries a group of highly religious residents. The religious norms and cultural pressures in the southern states, we assume, encourage newly arrived residents to also become more religious. A person who settles down in Vermont is likely to be less religious than if that same person settles down in Mississippi.

These state cultures are important for the future of religion. If a state with a highly religious culture grows, then the total number of highly religious people in the nation as a whole will grow as a result. If a state that is more nonreligious shrinks, it is contributing fewer and fewer of its less religious people to the national average. Some states are growing more than others. As we will see presently, the more religious states are growing the most. This potentially can have a significant effect on the overall religiousness of the U.S. in the years ahead.

## MISSISSIPPI ON TOP, VERMONT ON THE BOTTOM

Here are the specifics — the net religiousness of every state in the country using Gallup measures.

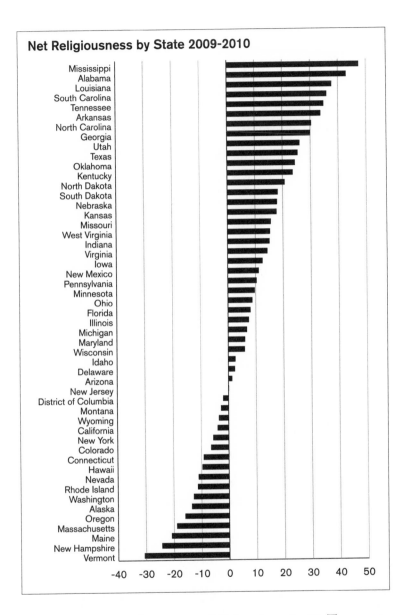

Net Religiousness by State 2009-2010

The average net religiousness of all Americans is +11. The average net religiousness of the different states varies a great deal around this mean, from a high of +48 in Mississippi to a low of -31 in Vermont.

These are huge differences. Mississippians are almost three times as likely to be in church on Sunday morning as Vermonters. There is a 43-point difference in self-reported importance of religion between residents of Vermont and residents of Mississippi.

A map of the 12 states with the highest average levels of religiousness, essentially the prototypical Bible Belt, in turn looks much like a map of the Confederacy 150 years ago. There were 11 Confederate states in the late Civil War (in order of secession, South Carolina, Mississippi, Florida, Alabama, Georgia, Louisiana, Texas, Virginia, Arkansas, Tennessee, and North Carolina). Nine of these states are among the top 10 most religious states in the country today. The only two Confederate states that don't make the religiousness cut are Florida and Virginia. The only non-Confederate state in the top 10 is Utah, which didn't exist as a state until 1896. The 11th and 12th most religious states are Oklahoma and Kentucky. Oklahoma did not exist as a state at the time of the Civil War, and Kentucky was close to being a Confederate state.

Seven of the 10 states that today have the lowest levels of religiousness were Union states (Vermont, New Hampshire, Maine, Massachusetts, Oregon, Rhode Island, and Nevada). The other three of the 10 states with the lowest levels of religiousness did not exist as states at the time of the Civil War (Washington, Alaska, and Hawaii).

Most of the highly religious states in the U.S. are in the South or close to the South. The least religious states in the U.S. tend to be in the Northeast or the West. Confederacy = religious states. Union and new states = less religious states.

The former Confederate states are of course more than just the most religious. They are also among today's most Republican states. The Union states of 150 years ago are not only today's least religious states, but they are also today's most Democratic states.

The continuing legacy of the Civil War is quite remarkable. There is so much geographic mobility, mass media, and mass culture that you would imagine that the United States would be very homogenous now that we are well into the 21$^{st}$ century. It's hard to believe that more than 230 years after the founding of the nation and more than 145 years after the Civil War, the states in the South still retain very distinctive cultural and political characteristics. But it's true.

## WHY THESE STATE-BY-STATE DIFFERENCES?

The states of the union vary substantially in terms of their residents' predominant brands of religion. Some states are highly Catholic; others have very few Catholics. Some are full of Protestants. One state is dominated by Mormons. People who identify with some religions are more religious than people who identify with others. Thus, one explanation for the state-by-state differences in religiousness focuses on differences in the religious composition of the states.

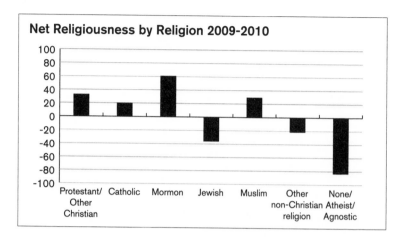

Here are the basic facts: Mormons get an extraordinary yield from their adherents. Protestants and Muslims do all right, followed by Catholics. Americans who identify their religion as Jewish simply do not attend religious services very often and are quite unlikely to say that religion is important in their daily lives.

Now the question is how much these different religiousness "yields" account for variation in the average religiousness of the states. If we find that the religious brand identity of a state's residents primarily drives that state's religiousness, then it throws water on the state culture theory. Let's see what the data show.

## PROTESTANTS

Fifty-four percent of Americans are Protestants. Everything else being equal, we would expect 54% of residents in every state to be Protestants. That's not the case. Protestants are dominant in southern states and rarer in the Northeast.

Alabama has a higher percentage of Protestant residents than any other state in the union — 80%. Another nine states have 71% or higher Protestant populations. All of these are in (or near) the South: Mississippi, Tennessee, Arkansas, South Carolina, Oklahoma, North Carolina, West Virginia, Georgia, and Kentucky.

Seven states have fewer than 40% Protestant residents: Rhode Island, Massachusetts, Connecticut, New Jersey, New York, New Hampshire, and Utah. With the exception of Utah, all are in the Middle Atlantic or New England regions.

Roger Finke and Rodney Stark detail some of the reasons why Protestants are so prevalent in the South in their book *The Churching of America: 1776-2005*. The U.S. began as a largely Protestant country. The South was affected by the waves of indentured slaves brought to the region but was not disrupted by large waves of other non-Protestant arrivals. There was fairly minimal immigration by Catholics and Jews into the South over the years. This meant that the South stayed Protestant. Plus, two dominant Protestant sects flourished in the South at the end of the 18th century — the Methodists and the Baptists, further ensuring that this region remained Protestant.

Keep in mind that Protestants are more religious than the national average. Protestants average +33 net religiousness. That's triple the national average of +11. This suggests that highly religious states in the South may be religious mostly because they contain a high percentage of naturally more religious Protestants. The data show, however, that there is more to it than this.

Taking Utah out of the picture, for reasons I will discuss shortly, I correlated the religiousness of the states based only on their Protestant residents with the list of states based only on non-Protestant residents. The resulting correlation coefficient is 0.65. This is fairly high. It tells us that a religious state is a religious state *regardless* of whether we look at that state's Protestant population or at its non-Protestant population. The religiousness of a state is *not solely* dependent on the percentage of Protestants in that state. Just to be clear on this point: This correlation exercise checks to see if the 50 states have similar levels of religiousness whether we look at Protestants or at non-Protestants. They do.

The residents of certain states — mainly in the South and Midwest — are highly religious regardless of whether we look only at Protestants or if we take Protestants out of the equation altogether and look only at non-Protestants. Mississippi, for example, is a highly religious state to a remarkable degree no matter which group of its residents we look at. Vermont is a nonreligious state no matter which group of its residents we look at. Non-Protestants in Mississippi average +15 net religiousness. Non-Protestants in Vermont average -45 net religiousness. Protestants in Mississippi have an average +56 net religiousness. Protestants in Vermont have an average -9 net religiousness. Something about states such as Mississippi leads to a situation in which their residents are highly religious — whether those residents happen to be Protestants or not. Something about states such as Vermont leads to a situation in which their residents are highly nonreligious — whether those residents happen to be Protestants or not.

I also conducted an analysis that ranked the states based only on the religiousness of the Protestants in each state. I removed everybody else from the picture. The top 10 most religious states, looking only at Protestant residents in all 50 states, are all in the

South. This is basically the same picture we get when we look at religiousness based on all residents in a state.

**Bottom line:** Mississippi is highly religious because it is Mississippi — not because there are a lot of Protestants living there.

## CATHOLICS

Catholics first came to this country through Eastern ports in the great migrations of the 1800s and early 1900s. Many settled and put down roots where they landed. That's why we find high Catholic populations in the Middle Atlantic and northeastern states.

A second wave of Catholic-oriented Hispanics from Mexico and Central America came into this country more recently. This explains why southwestern states — in particular Texas, California, and New Mexico — have a lot of Catholics. Before any of this occurred, French Canadian Catholics (the Cajuns), fled from what is now Nova Scotia and ended up in Louisiana, helping explain the relatively high Catholic percentage in that state today.

Rhode Island is the most Catholic state in the union (50% Catholic), while Alabama is the least Catholic state (7% Catholic). Six states in the U.S. today are more than one-third Catholic. All are on the mid to upper East Coast: Rhode Island, Massachusetts, New Jersey, Connecticut, New York, and New Hampshire. Four states are between 30% and 32% Catholic: Wisconsin, New Mexico, California, and Illinois.

Rhode Island, Massachusetts, New Jersey, Connecticut, New York, and to a degree New Hampshire are all close to the ports of entry for Catholics. New Mexico and California border Mexico and thus are ports of entry for the second wave of majority Catholic Hispanics. Wisconsin and Illinois, both higher than average Catholic, are not close to the ports of entry. Presumably, the higher Catholic percentages in these states represent migration patterns after Catholics arrived in this country.

At the other end of the spectrum are the 19 states with less than 19% Catholic population. There are six states with less than 10% Catholic population. All of these are in the South: Alabama, Mississippi, Tennessee, Arkansas, West Virginia, and South Carolina. Other states with 10% Catholic population include Utah, North Carolina, and Oklahoma. None of these states are close to the ports of entry for Catholics along the Atlantic, nor are they contiguous with Mexico.

That leaves 21 states and the District of Columbia that are within five points of the national average, including three states that are so average that their percentage Catholic is exactly the national average, at 24%: Michigan, Delaware, and Nebraska.

But not all Catholics are created equally. Remarkably, the state in which Catholics reside has a major impact on their religiousness. Catholics in highly religious states are themselves highly religious, while Catholics in less religious states are themselves less religious. Although you will have to look hard to find them, the relatively few Catholics in Mississippi are more religious than Catholics in any other state in the union — except for Louisiana. Catholics in Alabama are also highly religious. On the other hand, the large number of Catholics in Rhode Island and Massachusetts are among the *least* religious Catholics in the nation. The few Catholics in Vermont are second only to New Hampshire as being the least religious Catholics in the nation.

Overall, Catholics are slightly more religious than average, with a +20 net religiousness score compared with the national average of +11. But, we've seen little evidence that the concentration of Catholics in a particular state is at all related to the state's religiousness. Whether we look only at Catholics or only at non-Catholics, the same states rise to the top of our list based on religiousness.

In short, a state's relative religiousness affects *all* the residents of that state, including Catholics. Rhode Island Catholics are, relatively speaking, not very religious. Mississippi Catholics are quite a bit more religious than most other Catholics. The state's culture is what appears to matter, not the percentage of Catholics in that state. The correlation between the religiousness of the states based on Catholics only and the religiousness based only on non-Catholics is 0.77. The average religiousness of a state — the religious culture of the state — affects its Catholic residents, and it affects its non-Catholic residents. Catholics who move to Mississippi, in other words, in theory will become more religious than Catholics who move to Rhode Island or Vermont.

## THE FASCINATING CASE OF UTAH AND THE MORMONS

Mitt Romney's tax return for 2010, which he begrudgingly made public in January 2012, shows that he gave about $1.5 million to The Church of Jesus Christ of Latter-day Saints in that year. This huge contribution to his church underscores that Mitt Romney is very religious. It also reflects the fact that Mormons are very religious as a group, basically the most religious group in America. Mormons average a +61 net religiousness score. The average net religiousness score in the U.S. is +11. Thus, if a state has a lot of Mormons in it, we assume that could affect how religious the state is. That is in fact the case. This is the one instance where the religion of the residents of a state appears to drive that state's religiousness.

Based on Gallup survey calculations, about 1% of Americans aged 18 and older live in Utah, while 34% of the total Mormon population lives in Utah. Almost six out of 10 adults in Utah are Mormon, about 30 times the national average. At the other end of the spectrum, only 0.6% (that is one-sixth of a percent) of those living in North Dakota are Mormon. That's about one-twentieth of the national average. There is obviously a great deal of variation in the distribution of Mormons around the country.

The reasons for this are clear. The growth of the Mormon religion began in upstate New York. Led by Joseph Smith and then Brigham Young, Mormons fled various persecutions in New York, and then Illinois, and kept moving until they reached Utah, where they flourished and remain dominant. Mormons have spread out geographically to the states surrounding Utah (e.g., Idaho), reflecting the natural pattern by which people choose to move close by rather than far away. States not close to Utah have very few Mormons on a proportionate basis.

Utah is the ninth most religious state in the union. An extraordinary 77% of Mormons living in Utah are classified as very religious, almost twice the national average. However, and this is important, Utah's Mormons are not exceptional just because they live in Utah. They are generally no more or no less religious than Mormons anywhere else. There does not appear to be something about Utah's climate, topology, or latitude and longitude — or culture — that makes its residents more religious. Utah's residents are religious, it appears, because they are Mormon.

On the other hand, non-Mormons in Utah, about 44% of the state, are *not very religious at all* on a relative basis. Twenty-five percent of Utah's non-Mormons are very religious compared with 42% in the country as a whole, and 53% are not religious, well above the 30% national average. For the roughly four out of 10 Utahans who are not Mormon, something about the state appears to drive *down* religiousness — to one of the lowest rates in the country. It is unclear why this is the case. There could be a rebellion effect of some sort going on in Utah. Maybe those who are not Mormon react against the highly apparent religiousness of those who are. Or it could be that in recent years, people who are both non-Mormon and not very religious have moved to Utah for various nonreligious, presumably economic, reasons.

Utah does not seem to have a magic religious quality that affects residents who live there. Rather, Utah has a lot of highly religious, church-attending Mormons in its boundaries. *This makes Utah the exception to the general conclusion that a state's culture drives that state's religiousness.* If there is a state culture in Utah, it is one that causes non-Mormons to rebel against religion.

## NO RELIGIOUS IDENTITY

Americans who don't have any religious identity at all — including those who declare themselves atheists or agnostics — represent about 16% of the country's population. Everything else being equal, 16% of residents of every state should have no religious identity.

This is not the case. By now, this should come as no surprise; we have found "maldistribution" of every religious group we have looked at so far. The percentage of residents with no religious identity ranges from 25% in Oregon, 24% in Vermont, and 23% in Washington down to 6% in Mississippi and 7% in North Dakota, Alabama, and Louisiana.

The nine states with the highest "no religion" percentages (20% or higher) are: Oregon, Vermont, Washington, Alaska, Maine, Hawaii, New Hampshire, Colorado, and the District of Columbia. All of these states are in the West (including Hawaii and Alaska as part of the West) or in New England, except for the District of Columbia.

There are only seven states with less than 10% "no religion," and six of them are in the South: Mississippi, North Dakota, Louisiana, Alabama, Arkansas, Tennessee, and South Carolina. North Dakota is the one outlier in this group.

There isn't anything immediately apparent that explains why some states have more religiously unbranded residents than others. "Something in the water" drives people away from religion in New England states as well as in a number of very different states (at least geographically) in the West. Whatever causes people in certain states to declare they have no religious identity quite naturally causes them to be less religious on other dimensions as well.

This doesn't mean that the overall religious culture of a state has no impact on that state's residents. Religiousness varies across states whether we look at people with a religious identity or at those without. The "state culture" hypothesis appears to work its magic on all of a state's residents, even among those with no religious identity.

Sixteen percent of the residents of Mississippi with no religious identity *still* are classified as very religious. This is a low religiousness number on an absolute basis. But it is high on a relative basis because only 3% of those nationwide who have no religious identity are very religious. By contrast, only 1% of the residents of Vermont with no religious identity are very religious, and 93% are nonreligious. This is a low religiousness number on an absolute *and* relative basis.

In short, the few Mississippians who don't have a religious identity are much more religious than Vermonters who don't have a religious identity — by a big margin. *This is remarkable.* The religious culture of the state of Mississippi seems to affect everyone who lives in that state — even those who do not have a religious identity. The nonreligious culture in Vermont appears to affect everyone living in that state — regardless of their religious identity.

No matter who you are, I think it's likely that if you move to Mississippi, you will become more religious than if you move to Vermont. At least that's a viable hypothesis.

These results certainly add weight to the conclusion that states have powerful cultural differences that affect the religiousness of those living within their borders.

## ETHNICITY AND RACE

Blacks are by far the most religious race or ethnic group in the country. Mississippi, the most religious state in the union, has the highest percentage of black residents of any state (not counting the District of Columbia). Thirty-two percent of adult residents of Mississippi are black. By contrast, nonreligious states like Vermont, New Hampshire, and Oregon all have 1% or fewer black residents.

The presence of highly religious blacks in southern states would logically seem to be a factor in the South's generally high ranking on the scale of religious states. The absence of highly religious blacks in New England states like Vermont and New Hampshire could bring down their average religiousness scores.

However, the racial composition of a state is only a partial explanation for that state's religiousness. Once again, the religious culture of a state seems to have a powerful effect on everyone within that state's borders, regardless of their race or ethnicity.

Removing the influence of blacks within a state makes little difference in its relative religiousness. *The rank order of the religiousness of the states among whites only is virtually the same as the rank order when all residents are taken into account.* Whites in southern states are much more religious than whites in the Northeast and the West. White Mississippians are the most religious, followed by whites in Alabama, Tennessee, Arkansas, Louisiana, Utah, South Carolina, North Carolina, Oklahoma, and Georgia. Whites in Vermont, New Hampshire, Massachusetts, Maine, and the District of Columbia are the least religious.

And remarkably, the rank order of states based on how religious they are follows this same pattern when we isolate the black population. Blacks living in southern states are substantially more religious on average than blacks living in states in the Northeast and the West. The strongly religious cultures in southern states apparently affect the average religiousness of the black residents of those states just like they affect the religiousness of the white residents of those states. And the nonreligious cultures of Northeastern, Middle Atlantic, and Western states affect the average religiousness of black residents of those states. Blacks living in South Carolina are almost 40 times as religious as blacks living in Rhode Island.

*All in all, the race and ethnic composition of a state does not appear to go very far in explaining variations in the state's religiousness.* Residents of southern states appear to be religious whatever their ethnicity or race, while residents of states in the Northeast, Middle Atlantic, and the West are nonreligious regardless of their ethnicity or race.

## THE SCOOP ON STATE CULTURES

The cultures of the 50 states of the union obviously have a significant influence on the religious attitudes and behavior of their residents.

As I have noted, states with a highly religious culture have residents who tend to be religious regardless of their religious identity or ethnicity. States with a less religious culture include residents who tend to be less religious regardless of their religious identity or ethnicity.

In fact, a multivariate statistical analysis confirms that an American's state of residence remains an important predictor variable of that person's religiousness, even when taking into account a whole list of other variables that could also be related to religiousness. Something about certain states simply seems to affect the religiousness of those therein. In other words, no matter what else I know about you and your demographic characteristics, knowing what state you live in provides a little extra "predictive power" in guessing how religious you are.

That leaves us with perhaps the most interesting questions of all: Why are certain regions of the country less religious than others? Why are the New England states of Vermont, New Hampshire, Maine, and Massachusetts and the Western states of Alaska, Oregon, Washington, Nevada, Montana, and Hawaii so low on the religiousness scale? I'm not sure there is one easy answer to these questions. But it does appear that each state has unique norms and cultures that arise from that state's history and that in turn affect those who live there.

Alaska is one of the least religious states in the country. It certainly has a unique state culture. John McPhee's classic 1977 book *Coming Into the Country* describes to great effect the iconoclastic residents of our 49th state. Many of these people moved to Alaska specifically to get away from normality, conformity, and the strictures of the "lower 48." Loners, eccentrics, misanthropes of all types chose Alaska specifically because it offered the promise of an out-of-the-way, isolated existence. Few of these people appear to have been classically religious. Alaska's culture includes a lot of things, but religion is not one of them.

Vermont is associated with stoic, self-sufficient, perhaps hippie-like virtues. It is a state with weather and geographical extremes — cold weather, snow, and lots of rugged territory and mountains. There are no large cities. People in the state — I think it's fair to say — are more likely to be loners than people in other states. Although it's hard to pinpoint exact evidence of the relationship between these virtues and the absence of religion among Vermonters, I think it's logical that there is a connection.

Mississippi is a classically "Deep South" state with few geographic or weather challenges — save the hurricanes that periodically ravage the Gulf Coast. Mississippi is generally flat. If there is a weather problem, it is the heat and humidity of the summer. The Southern culture of the state embraces charm, sociability, graces, social standing, social and racial hierarchies, norms dictating appropriate behavior, and folksiness. And the Southern culture of Mississippi embraces religion, helping make it the most religious state in the union.

Living in Mississippi is simply a different experience than living in Vermont or Alaska. All of these states have different cultures — learned patterns of behaviors in given situations that exist before, during, and after the life of any one individual. These rules of behavior and approaches to life can be powerful. They certainly appear to affect the politics of the various states. Mississippi is one of the reddest states in the union while Vermont is one of the bluest. These state cultures appear to affect those living in a state and presumably will affect those who choose to migrate into a state.

I did look at one specific aspect of a state's culture I thought might help explain the differences — marital status. As I will discuss in Chapter VII, married Americans are more religious than those who are single, and in particular, more religious than those living with domestic partners. If Vermont is full of single people or those living with domestic partners, this could help explain their lack of religion. Perhaps southern states are, by contrast, full of married people — and this helps explain those states' high levels of religiousness.

I don't see much support for these hypotheses. First of all, there isn't a lot of variation in marital status across the states. The majority of states cluster fairly closely to the overall mean of 50% of adults who were married at the time they were interviewed and 4% who report living with a domestic partner.

For example, half of the residents of Vermont we interviewed are married. Slightly less than half (45%) of those in Mississippi are married. Four percent of Americans said they are living with a domestic partner, and 4% are living with a domestic partner in Vermont, almost exactly the same as the percentage in Mississippi.

Second, we find that married people and single people in Mississippi are more religious than married people and single people in Vermont. Louisiana has one of the lowest marriage rates in the country, yet it is one of the most religious states. There just doesn't seem to be compelling evidence that differences in the culture of marriage in the states are highly related to differences in religiousness.

---

## Bottom Line

What are the implications of the differing state cultures of religion? States appear to have religious cultures all their own — cultures that dictate how religious their residents are — above and beyond any other factors. As a result, some states are highly religious, and some states are not very religious at all. If highly religious states gain residents over time, and if low-religious state lose residents, the total number of religious people in the U.S. could increase.

There are significant differences in the relative growth of the 50 states. While the United States added more than 27 million people between 2000 and 2010, one state — Michigan — actually lost population over that decade. Another state — Nevada — increased its population by 35% over the same time period.

I looked at the 10 states that gained the most in population on a proportionate basis between 2000 and 2010. The average net religiousness score for those 10 states is +14.26. Then I looked at the 10 states that gained the least in terms of population between 2000 and 2010. The average net religiousness for those states is +1.99, much lower than the top 10 gaining states.

Texas, California, Arizona, Florida, Georgia, and North Carolina had the largest absolute gains in population between 2000 and 2010. Georgia, North Carolina, and Texas are also well above average in terms of religiousness. If migration continues to these states, and if the religious culture of these states affects newly arrived residents, there could be an increase in religiousness therein. States that grew the least over the last decade include a number of less religious states, including Massachusetts, Michigan, New Jersey, and New York.

There are exceptions, of course. California and Arizona are below average in terms of religiousness and have enjoyed increasing populations — although the population increase in California appears to have slowed way down. More migration to those states could decrease average religiousness.

Let's look at 2000-2010 population gains in the 10 states that are the most religious and in the 10 states that are the least religious. The 10 most religious states gained 9.8 million people from 2000 to

2010. The 10 least religious states gained just 2.5 million people. So, at least as of the last U.S. Census, highly religious states appear to be gaining more population on average than highly nonreligious states.

**Population gain, 10 most religious states, 2000-2010**

|  | Population gain | Net religiousness |
|---|---|---|
| Texas | 4,293,741 | 25.50 |
| Utah | 530,716 | 26.20 |
| Georgia | 1,501,200 | 30.00 |
| North Carolina | 1,486,170 | 30.40 |
| Arkansas | 242,518 | 33.80 |
| Tennessee | 656,822 | 34.90 |
| South Carolina | 613,352 | 36.00 |
| Louisiana | 64,396 | 37.80 |
| Alabama | 332,636 | 43.00 |
| Mississippi | 122,639 | 47.50 |
| **Total gain** | **9,844,190** | |

**Population gain, 10 least religious states, 2000-2010**

|  | Population gain | Net religiousness |
|---|---|---|
| Vermont | 16,914 | -30.70 |
| New Hampshire | 80,684 | -24.40 |
| Maine | 53,438 | -20.90 |
| Massachusetts | 198,532 | -19.00 |
| Oregon | 409,675 | -16.00 |
| Alaska | 83,299 | -13.60 |
| Washington | 830,419 | -12.90 |
| Rhode Island | 4,248 | -11.40 |
| Nevada | 702,294 | -11.10 |
| Hawaii | 148,764 | -9.70 |
| **Total gain** | **2,528,267** | |

The long-term effect of these patterns of movement between states depends on how they change in the years to come. California is a major question because it has by far the largest population of any state. It is also less religious than many other states. If California begins to lose people or to lose people at a disproportionate rate and these people move to highly religious states, then the overall religiousness of the nation as a whole could increase. Migration patterns into and out of religious and nonreligious states will clearly have an effect on the nation's future religiousness.

# CHAPTER VII

## Men and Women

*American women of all ages and all social positions find religion more important and worship more frequently than their male counterparts.*

Eighty-five-year-old women are more religious than 85-year-old men. Twenty-year-old women are more religious than 20-year-old men.

This seemingly inevitable and universal gender gap occurs in almost all countries around the world. Gallup research identifies only 15 countries out of 153 included in recent surveys in which men are more religious than women.

These differences are not new. We can observe this same gender gap going back in time for as long as Gallup has conducted surveys. Anecdotally, the gender bias in religiosity appears to have been around for as long as there has been recorded history.

Religion advocates face the challenge of explaining why God would smile more on women than men or why women would be more receptive to his message. Religion cynics face the challenge of explaining why women would be more "delusional" than men. Within the confines of this book, my questions are slightly different. What do we learn from the fact that women are universally more religious than men in America today? What does this seemingly inevitable and universal pattern tell us about religion and its future?

Scholars have developed theories to explain the religious gender gap. Some focus on the role that women have traditionally played — in charge of child rearing and thus presumably focused on the nurturing, "softer" side of life, including religion. Others argue that women are less likely to be in the workforce and more likely to have time for religion. Some simply argue that it is history and tradition — or as sociologists put it, socialization.

The most provocative explanations are biological in nature — focusing on the evolutionary benefit that accrues from women having more of an interest in religion than men. Is it possible that it has been evolutionarily adaptive throughout history for men to take risks and eschew the security religion brings? Or, is religion an adaptive response by women to centuries of oppression and subjugation to subordinate roles within the social matrix?

There is a growing divide in the role that women play in religious groups. In many mainline Protestant denominations today, clergy and leadership roles are increasingly filled by women. On the other hand, many other religions — including Catholic, Muslim, and evangelical Protestant faiths — deny women access to the higher religious positions in their organizations. What are the implications of the fact that women are likely to dominate leadership in some religions in the years ahead while being denied full access to leadership in others?

The role of women in American society — in relationship to marriage, children, education, and employment — continues to change. These changes may have a significant effect on the overall patterns of religion in the U.S. in the years ahead.

## MEN'S HISTORIC DOMINATION

The world's major religions have historically been male-centric. Jesus, Buddha, Mohammed, Abraham — all were male. Of course, this reflected the points in time when these religions developed, when almost all societal institutions — political, economic, family — were male-centric. Times have changed in many ways. Today we have women heads of state, women CEOs of corporations, and women leaders in the military. Many religions have female leadership as well. But this is by no means universal. While a woman will be welcomed as a pastor in the United Methodist Church, she will find a closed door if she seeks to be a priest in the Catholic church or a minister in many conservative non-Catholic Christian denominations. The Southern Baptists, the country's largest Protestant denomination, have made this explicit in their Baptist Faith and Message statement: "While both men and women are gifted for service in the church, the office of pastor is limited to men as qualified by Scripture."

Yet, in America today, women are more religious than their male counterparts in almost all religions, regardless of the religion's position on women as clergy. This universal gender gap in religion seems to be as fundamental as the biological differences that distinguish the genders. It persists across age, socio-economic, ethnic, and regional groupings. The gender gap has apparently been with us for as long as we have recorded data. And, it appears to be a constant of life in the vast majority of countries around the world.

Explaining seemingly inevitable social facts has always been difficult for social scientists. Some social scientists do not like to think that *any* social facts are inevitable. Many scholars shy away from any hint that there might be a biological basis for gender (or race) differences because that implies that these differences cannot be easily changed or that they have a legitimate reason for being. On the other hand, much of the exciting current research in human behavior deals with a focus on just that — explanations for differences that focus on their development through evolution.

## THE BASICS

Gallup asked more than 700,000 people in 2009 and 2010 if religion was an important part of their daily lives and about their church attendance. The results, combined into our basic religiousness index, are as follows:

**Religiousness by Gender 2009-2010**

|        | Very Religious | Moderately Religious | Nonreligious |
|--------|:--------------:|:--------------------:|:------------:|
| Men    | 37%            | 27%                  | 36%          |
| Women  | 46%            | 29%                  | 25%          |

Not all women are religious, and not all men are nonreligious. We don't have a country of devout women coexisting with a nation of atheistic men. But the gender gap is statistically and reliably evident. Women are nine points more prevalent in the very religious group and 11 points less prevalent in the nonreligious group.

This same gender gap appears on almost any measure of religion one can think of. A few years ago, Gallup researcher Al Winseman reviewed gender differences on a number of indicators. Women were more religious than men in terms of being a member of a church or synagogue, saying that religion can answer today's problems, reading the Bible weekly, participating in Bible study groups, and paying attention to God in making decisions rather than paying attention to one's own views. Other studies show gender differences in self-reported prayer.

These results are of course not shockingly new. Anyone who attends church notes the preponderance of females in attendance. But the appearance of the gender gap across all these measures of religion underscores its robustness.

## HOW LONG HAS THIS BEEN GOING ON?

We don't have survey data that give us good estimates of the relative religiosity of men and women throughout history. Lamentably, our survey data go back only 70 years or so. But, these data certainly have shown conclusively that the gender gap was alive and well at least as far back as the late 1940s.

In 1947, Gallup asked Americans if they had gone to church the previous Sunday; 42% of men said they had, compared with 47% of women. In a 1950 Gallup poll, the difference in self-reported church attendance within the last seven days had grown to 10 points: 34% men and 44% women. In 1954, it was 42% men and 50% women. A

Gallup compilation of surveys during 1955 found that 43% of men on average and 54% of women said they had attended church in the last seven days. Skipping to 1966, it was 39% men and 49% women.

A Gallup survey from 1975 found that 47% of men said that their religious beliefs were very important, compared with 66% of women. In 1993, it was 53% of men saying very important and 65% of women saying very important. And so forth.

A look at the NORC GSS data shows the same historical patterns. The first GSS survey, conducted in 1972, found that 42% of women interviewed said they attended religious services every week or more than every week. By comparison, the percentage for men was 29%.

Surveys are by far our best mechanism for measuring society-wide traits such as the relationship between gender and religiousness. But lacking good surveys, there is other historical evidence that tends to support the idea of a gender gap "way back when." As one scholar described religion in colonial life: "New England women tended to join the church in greater numbers than men, a phenomenon known as the 'feminization' of religion, although it is not clear how that came about. In general, colonial women fared well for the times in which they lived. In any case the lead in the family practice of religion in New England was often taken by the wife. It was the mother who brought up the children to be good Christians, and the mother who often taught them to read so that they could study the Bible. Because both men and women were required to live according to God's law, both boys and girls were taught to read the Bible."

Other historical research reflects the same pattern. It seems reasonable to assume that although men were the religious leaders in times gone by, women may have been the most religious.

## AROUND THE WORLD

Visit almost any country in the world, and you are likely to find that the women in that country — regardless of its dominant religion — are more religious than their male counterparts. This religious gender gap is certainly not just an American phenomenon.

Gallup has conducted interviews in more than 150 countries around the world in recent years. In each interview, respondents were asked if religion was an important part of their daily life. In 127 out of 153 of these countries, women were more likely, on average, to say "yes" to the religion question than were men. In another 11 countries, men and women were equal on the religious importance dimension. In only 15 countries were women less likely than men to say religion is important.

The gender gap is largest in Argentina, where 67% of women said that religion is important, compared with 43% of men. Other countries with a gender gap of 20 percentage points or more include Bulgaria, Belarus, Lithuania, and Portugal.

The countries in which there is a reverse gender gap — men more likely than women to say religion is important — tend to be those where religion is very important to everyone. For example, in Thailand, 100% of men said that religion is important, compared with 99% of women — a reverse gender gap to be sure, but not substantially significant. Similarly, in Egypt, 99% of men said religion is important compared with 97% of women; in the Comoros, it was 99% for men, 98% for women; and in Cambodia, it was 96% for men and 94% for women. The country with the highest reverse gender gap is Kyrgyzstan, where 69% of men said religion is important, contrasted with 60% of women — a function of the unusual history and culture of that country.

The Scandinavian countries of Finland, Norway, Sweden, and Denmark are among the least religious in the world. Why that's the case is the topic for another book. Yet in each of these countries, women are more religious than men. For example, in Finland, 18% of men said religion is important compared with 34% of women; Norway, 16% and 25%; Sweden, 13% and 18%; and Denmark, 16% and 19%. Religion is also not very important overall in Hong Kong and China. But women are more likely to say religion is important than are men in both.

As is the case for the U.S. data, the gender gap differences in many countries of the world are not extreme. But they underscore the remarkable pattern of underlying regularity in religious consciousness by gender we find across geography, culture, and dominant religion.

## ARTIFACT OF AGE?

Women are more religious than men at *all* ages. The religious gender gap in the U.S. begins early in life and continues until Americans are at death's doorstep. Your 20-year-old daughter is likely to be more religious than your 20-year-old son. And your 85-year-old grandmother is likely to be more religious than your

85-year-old grandfather. There are slight differences in the gender gap across age groups, but nothing substantively significant.

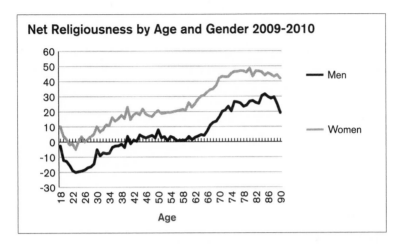

Look how very basic this relationship is. By age 18, when Gallup first interviews Americans, young women are more religious than young men. These teenagers are coming out of similar adolescent experiences as they begin to leave the home and enter the real world. Most of them don't have children and are not married — two variables highly related to religiousness. But this doesn't seem to matter. The gender gap appears so early in life that as soon as we can interview them, females report a higher degree of personal religious importance and more frequent church attendance than males.

I am personally intrigued by the finding that very old women are more religious than very old men. You might think that by the time Americans reach the senior stages of life, the increasing importance of religion in their lives might have wiped out gender differences. But that is not so. Even near the end of their lives, older women remain reliably more religious than older men.

I find all of this to be one of the most remarkable findings in this book. Just as physicists, chemists, and astronomers often look with wonder at the physical world they behold, I look with wonder at this representation of the social world. Our data reflect hundreds of thousands of separate, individual interviews conducted over a two-year period. Each person of all ages is independently asked about religion. Still, when all is said and done, American women at every age point from 18 through 90 are reliably more religious than men at the same ages. The symmetry and regularity in this pattern is indeed spectacular.

## THE GENDER GAP IN RACE, ETHNIC, AND RELIGIOUS IDENTITY GROUPS

So far, we have seen that:

1. Women are more religious than men in America today.

2. The gender gap appears as soon as women and men are old enough to be included in Gallup surveys — and it continues even among the oldest Americans we reach.

3. The gender gap has been evident as far back as we have had surveys about religion in the U.S.

4. The gender gap appears to have existed in some form in prior centuries in the U.S.

5. The gender gap exists across most countries worldwide.

Let's add to our knowledge now by probing how far the gender gap extends into the depths of the American population.

## Race and Ethnicity

Blacks, whites, Hispanics, and Asians come from different backgrounds and have different socialization patterns. They certainly have different positions and statuses in the American social and cultural system. It would not be unreasonable if males and females related differently to religion within each of these groups.

But, they don't. The overall gender gap in religiousness appears in *all* major race and ethnic groups in the U.S. White women are more religious than white men. Black women are more religious than black men. Hispanic women are more religious than Hispanic men. And Asian women are more religious than Asian men. The gender gap in religiousness is largest among blacks and Hispanics and smallest among Asians. Yet — and this is the key point — women are more religious than men in each ethnic group.

## Religious Brands

Groups of Americans who identify as Catholics, Protestants, other Christians, Jews, other non-Christian religions, and those with no religion are very different from one another. They have different traditions, different holy books, different authority structures, different outlooks on life, and different historical origins and patterns.

Some religions — namely Catholics and more conservative Protestant groups — explicitly treat women very differently than men. Catholics will not allow women into the priesthood. Many evangelical Christian denominations take quite seriously the apostle

Paul's admonition in I Timothy 2:12: "I do not permit a woman to teach or to exercise authority over a man; rather, she is to remain quiet." Other religions today are quite happy to accept women as clergy. In some Protestant denominations, in fact, the feminization of the clergy is so prevalent that women are fast becoming the majority of their ministers and pastors.

It certainly wouldn't be outrageous to hypothesize that the gap in religiousness between men and women would differ across these religious groups. But, again, it just isn't so. The gender gap in religiosity is front and center in all but one of the major religious groups we identify in our data.

Catholics are a particularly interesting case. We might guess that Catholic women could be demoralized by the rules prohibiting them from being priests and thus drift away from their religion. In fact, if religious women are leaving the Catholic church altogether, we would no longer identify them as Catholic in our surveys. But among men and women who continue to identify as Catholic, the evidence is clear: Catholic women are more likely to be religious than Catholic men, to the tune of a 19-point gender gap in net religiousness. The male-dominated hierarchy in the Catholic church doesn't appear to negatively affect the religiousness of female parishioners.

Non-Catholic Christians? A 14-point gender gap in religiousness. Jews are not very religious, regardless of gender. But, the data show — as should not be surprising by now — that Jewish women are more religious than Jewish men by seven points on the religiousness scale. Among those who identify with "other religions," women are also more religious than men.

Naturally enough, Americans with no religious identity are on average not very likely to say that religion is important in their daily life or to attend church. Still, women who have no religious identity are about four points higher on the religiousness scale than are men who have no religious identity.

The one exception to this pattern occurs among Muslim Americans. Muslim men have higher average levels of religiousness than do Muslim women. It is easy to point to the nature of the Islamic religion's theology and the Quran as the basis for the reverse gender gap among Muslims. But other religions — and the Bible — have theological bases that favor men, and in those religions, women are still more religious than men. The Muslim exception in this country is most likely related to elements of Muslim culture.

## EXPLANATIONS AND THEORIES FOR THE RELIGIOUS CONSCIOUSNESS GENDER GAP

At this point, we come back to two fundamental questions: Why are women more religious than men? And is this likely to change in the future?

I am not the first person to ask these questions. Maybe you have pondered this issue yourself. The answers run the gamut from theories relating to child rearing, to genetic/biological differences, to attempts by males to marginalize women, to historic norms, to the propensity of men to take more risks than women, to vestiges of older patriarchal cultures.

There is often no easy answer to the question of why *any* two groups are different from one another. There are usually a number of plausible explanations. And without experimental, controlled tests, the attempt to prove any of the explanations presents a devilish challenge.

For one thing, contemplating the religious gender gap brings up the *nature versus nurture* distinction that we find in many discussions of group differences. How much of the gender gap we see today in religiosity could be the result of nature (genetics and biology), and how much could be the result of nurture (environment)?

Sociologists often refer to the *nurture* part of the equation as *socialization* — the term for the learning that takes place after a person's birth as he or she moves through a particular set of social and cultural circumstances. An emphasis on socialization implies that women learn to be more religious than men. In this context, and in almost any context where there are social group differences on dimensions of interest, the nurture perspective leads to the conclusion that women are not born with, but acquire — from their culture or from the social systems in which they live — a higher religious consciousness than do men.

The *nature* perspective is based on the obvious fact that women are demonstrably different from men in their biology. Women have different genes and different biological wiring than men. The idea that physiological gender differences would be accompanied by more psychological, attitudinal differences is as old as Adam and Eve and appears again and again in popular culture ("men are from Mars, women are from Venus"), if not in most people's views of the world.

It is worth noting that any explanation for group differences focusing on nature can be controversial. Biologist Edward O. Wilson found this out in the 1970s when he published a massive book (*Sociobiology*) reviewing evidence suggesting that many social patterns had a biological, evolutionary basis. His critics did not like this viewpoint because it implied that group differences are inevitable and therefore can't be easily changed. While making a speech shortly after his book was published, angry critics poured water over Wilson's head. These critics hated the implication that biology or evolution had anything to do with social inequalities. (I will forge ahead nonetheless and hopefully avoid this same fate).

At least by my way of thinking, neither the socialization nor the biological way of looking at the world is an explanation in and of itself. Both require investigating *root causes* of the gender gap in religious consciousness — whether genetic or cultural.

We presume that even if the gender gap evolved, there had to be a reason for it — just like we assume there are reasons why men evolved to be taller on average than women. Evolutionary differences have to come from somewhere. If men and women are wired in a way that alters their relative probability of becoming religious, there should be a reason why this is evolutionarily beneficial. Somewhere back in the history of human evolution, these biological differences happened — we assume — because they made sense for the survival of the species.

There also has to be a reason if the gender gap developed because of human action. If women are taught to be more religious than men, the question remains: Why? Why have cultural norms and social patterns developed that favor religion for females more than for males? Socialization patterns do not exist in a vacuum. These patterns presumably developed because they made sense — if not for society as a whole, then for particular groups in power.

So I think we are left with the same question in either case: *Why* did the culture *and/or* biology develop to the point where we find near universal differences in the religiousness of men and women?

Some highly religious people may want to assume, of course, that the reasons are directly related to God's plan. Could it be that in his wisdom, God *selectively* makes himself known to groups of people on earth? Has God, in his (her?) infinite wisdom, simply made the decision to smile on women and reveal himself to them more than he does to men?

I call this the "differential divine selection assumption." Could it be that God picks and chooses the individuals he wants to receive the truth of his existence? God chose Mary to be the mother of Jesus and intervened in Saul's life on the road to Damascus, as represented in the book of Acts in the New Testament. God appears to have favored Abel over his brother Cain as related in the book of Genesis in the Old Testament. God chose to save Noah's life when the big flood came.

So, it is *possible* that God makes himself known more to women than to men. If so, it raises interesting questions for religious fundamentalists who have to deal with a situation in which God made women more religious, but in their view, designated that only men could be religious leaders. At any rate, in the final analysis, we simply don't have a scientific way to test the degree to which the gender gap in the U.S. today is the direct result of divine intervention — at least to my knowledge. So, we are back to more secular explanations.

## IS THE GENDER GAP FUNCTIONAL FOR SOCIETY?

A good starting point is to assume that group differences exist for a reason. That is, social systems develop patterns and structures because they help the systems function. This represents a "functionalist" approach to understanding society.

All social systems have structures, practices, and normative patterns that exist before and after any given individual moves through them. That's the essence of a sociological approach to human society. People come. People go. But from womb to tomb, people come and go through a set of social structures that have, in essence, a life of their own. These include the family, religious organizations and institutions, social status strata, educational systems, business institutions, racial and ethnic groupings, sexual norms, and finally, funeral and end-of-life customs.

Regarding religion, we find that in the U.S. (and apparently in much of the world), these social systems developed such that as people are born, grow up, and die, women on average are predisposed to have a higher religious consciousness than men. A functionalist approach assumes this happens for a reason.

Here is a parallel example: We know there are great differences in how the things people value are distributed in a society (i.e., inequality). Functionalist theorists argue that this inequality exists because it must be good for society — in other words, high levels of rewards attract the most talented to the most difficult roles, thus benefiting everyone.

I will remind you that this line of thought is often quite controversial. In the 2012 presidential campaign, the whole arena of the appropriate degree of inequality in society became a major topic of debate. President Obama called for extracting more taxes from higher income Americans. Occupy Wall Street groups protested in New York City and elsewhere against wealthy corporations and wealthy individuals. Obama and the Occupy protestors were wholeheartedly arguing that inequality was not functional — but dysfunctional — for society. Conservatives, on the other hand, made the argument that inequality *was* functional, that it was good for society to have highly attractive rewards awaiting those who worked hard and created jobs.

Social scientists with a functionalist orientation believe that religion is an essential part of integration, pattern maintenance, and relationship building. Religion is seen as a binding force that helps social systems maintain internal cohesion, provide meaning to the enterprise, and provide a legitimating authority to justify and explain normative and structural patterns in the society. It helps members of the population ease through the transition points of a social system, acting as a soothing force at times of disruption, sorrow, and stresses on the system. Religion provides an overarching presence at births, coming-of-age ceremonies, weddings, and deaths. And religion helps maintain relationships among members of a team or social system.

Division of labor is an efficient way to see that these integrative functions of religion are fulfilled. Division of labor systems in most societies have been — at least partially — based on gender. Males focus more on goal attainment and adaptation, while females focus more on integration and pattern maintenance. This generally is how societies have operated for thousands of years. Hence, the argument goes, women have evolved, either culturally or biologically, to take on the work focused on a social system's integrative functions. These in turn are highly related to religion. This explains the fact that women have higher degrees of religious consciousness than men.

As George Gallup Jr., son of the founder of Gallup, wrote a few years ago: "Historically, differing social roles may have encouraged greater religious participation among women: for example, mothers have tended to spend more time than fathers in raising and nurturing their children — which has often included overseeing their involvement in church activities."

The Shaker societies in New York and the Midwest were opposed to sexual relations, which was fine until their group literally died out. This was not a very functional system. Societies must replace members who die. Women are integral to fulfilling this function. They have the biological responsibility of bringing children into the world. In many cultures, women take on the bulk of the children's socialization responsibilities as well. Women have a genetic inclination to care for newborn babies.

If we assume that religion exists to help a society with its need for integration and pattern maintenance, then we could reasonably expect that those who are traditionally more involved in one of the most important of these functions — child rearing — to be more religious.

Plus, perhaps something about the magic of having a baby and bonding so closely with her child increases a woman's appreciation for the awesomeness of life — which in turn increases a woman's probability of integrating a religious perspective into her life.

It is extremely tricky to try to prove any of this. I think it's possible that in the future, scientists may be able to study the physiological changes that occur in various brain functions after a woman has a child and then perhaps relate those to the propensity to be religious. But for now, we can look at survey data that relate gender, marriage, children, and religion. It is particularly interesting to see if we can connect the clear finding that women are more religious with the clear finding that women have the biological responsibility for bearing, delivering, and initially caring for children.

The accompanying graph shows that women aged 18 to 44 with a child in the home are the most religious, at all ages. They are followed by men with children, then women with no children, and then finally, men with no children.

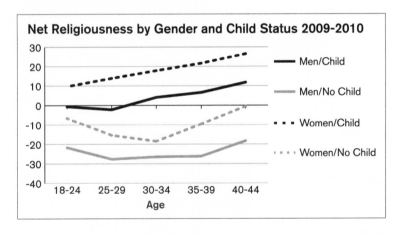

So, *women with children* **are** *more religious than women without children, regardless of age.* This supports the idea that having a child may highlight, accelerate, or bring prominence to the underlying religious instinct that women have because of their biology. When a woman has a child, the maternal instinct and the religion that goes with it may be accelerated. But, and this is the confounding fact, *men*

*have a similar "children gap."* At all age groups, *men* with a child in the home are more religious than men without a child in the home.

These findings certainly confirm one thing: *People who have a child have higher levels of religious consciousness than people of the same age who do not have a child.* In and of itself, this undergirds the idea that religion is related to some of the wondrous events that occur in people's lives.

Our interest here, however, is the gender gap in religion. The effect of having a child in the home is clearly evident among men *and* women. There is little evidence that having a child is more associated with a woman's religious consciousness than it is with a man's. Both genders appear to be affected more or less equally.

It is possible that people who are more religious to begin with are more likely to decide to have children. But because the correlation is evident among men and women, this view also does not help us answer the basic question of why women are more religious than men. *In short, we cannot prove with these data that having a child creates some unusual religious response among women that is not created among men.*

This is only one way of looking at the possible relationship between the biological fact that women have babies and the social fact that women are more religious. Biologists and psychologists may come up with other more complex methods in the future.

## CONFLICT THEORY: THE GENDER GAP HELPS THOSE IN POWER

Are you a cynic or dyed-in-the-wool critic who usually assumes the worst when it comes to your fellow humans? If so, you will appreciate another approach to differences in society — one that is premised on the assumption that life is a big conflict in which some groups of people are constantly trying to get ahead on the backs of other people.

This is a quite different viewpoint from the one held by functionalists. Functionalist theorists say social arrangements arise over time because they benefit the entire society. Conflict theorists believe social arrangements exist because powerful people arrange them to benefit themselves. To be sure, I am doing some major "shorthanding" in my descriptions. Social science theories are very complex, often too much so. Those who immerse themselves in certain theoretical approaches to society often make them extremely complicated. Heated arguments about nuances and splitting hairs result. Hopefully, my descriptions make the bases of these theories clear, even knowing that a hundred scholars would describe them in a hundred different ways.

In an Agatha Christie murder mystery, the detective often starts investigating a case by asking, "Cui bono?" (Who benefits?) The most likely suspect is often the person who benefitted most from the victim's demise. In conflict theory, the reasoning is much the same. Seeking an explanation for a social arrangement, one asks, "Who benefits?" Generally, this approach argues that those with the power benefit from existing arrangements, and therein lies the explanation for why they exist.

Take, for example, the pre-Civil War South. Someone was benefitting from that region's system of slavery, but obviously, it was not the slaves. The people who were benefitting were those who held the power — the plantation owners and others who made their living off the fruits of the slave-worked land. Clearly, the slave society was not functional for *all* of society, but for smaller segments of society.

This is an extreme example, but it underscores the point. Societal arrangements do not always develop because they are good for everyone in society. They also develop because people in power set things up so that they benefit the people in power — not society as a whole.

The most famous conflict theorist was Karl Marx. He believed that those who own the means of production arrange the rest of society so that they can continue to enjoy the fruits of their ownership. In fact, Marx argued that humans' "consciousness" itself developed out of the need of those with the power to maintain existing arrangements. Hence, "false" consciousness described a situation in which a person's brain was co-opted and the individual duped into thinking that his or her terrible lot in life was normal. That is to say, business as usual.

Religion, in Marx's view, was a specific form of false consciousness. Religion ("the opium of the people") was designed to help subjugate the masses, pacify them, and keep them placidly obedient to the existing arrangement of society, which of course benefitted those with the power/the bourgeoisies/those who own the means of production.

Marx's theories were extreme, but conflict theorists would view the gender gap in religious consciousness from a similarly critical perspective. The gender gap in religion exists in part, they would say, because of power arrangements in society. Women are more religious because that was (or is) useful to those with the power.

Or, women became more religious because they didn't have power — which they demonstrably did not in most societies until things began to change in more recent times.

The situation involving blacks in U.S. society provides an obvious parallel, which I discussed in Chapter IV. Blacks today are significantly more religious than whites. This enhanced religious consciousness in part, conflict theorists would argue, developed out of the centuries of black oppression and slavery. A high religious consciousness, with its emphasis on the rewards waiting in the "sweet by and by" (heaven) provided black slaves with a respite from the horrors of daily existence — and was often encouraged by slave owners.

A conflict orientation to the gender gap in religion follows this same line of thought. Women became the more religious of the genders because they were the least powerful of the genders.

The differences between the functionalist and conflict approaches are mainly a matter of interpretation. The first argues, in essence, that differences in religiousness by gender developed because they make society work better. The second argues that differences developed as a reaction to power arrangements in society.

These ways of contemplating gender differences are thought-provoking. But they are devilishly hard to test, as I have noted previously. Still, if power is important as an explanation for the gender gap in religiousness, it's useful to look at data we have that address these issues. In particular, I think we can learn from studying the relationship between some measures of women's orientation to power — income, education, employment status, marriage — and religiousness.

Our hypothesis is that women who have achieved high statuses should be *less* religious than women who have not. Why? Because high levels of formal education or income, in theory, give women more power. With that power *could* come less of a need for religion. In other words, if women develop higher religious consciousness as part of a need to cope with their less powerful status, women who have more power would need religion less.

## Income

Religiousness drops slightly as income increases for both genders. However, women are significantly more religious than men at *all* levels of income. The size of the gender gap in religiousness gets only slightly smaller as income increases. These are not huge differences.

And, for our purposes, *the key finding is that the religiousness gender gap exists across all levels of income.* Being relatively well-off apparently does not inoculate women from the overall tendency to be more religious than men.

## Education

A conflict theory approach would argue that women with higher educational status would be less likely to be religious. We *do* find support for this idea in the data. Net religiousness begins to drift down among women as education increases. At the same time, it's a much more mixed pattern *among men*, with no linear pattern as education increases. In fact, the religiousness gap between women and men goes from 24 points among those with less than a high school education to seven points among those with a postgraduate education.

So, although women are more religious than men at all levels of education, the gender gap shrinks among highly educated Americans. In short, a female Ph.D. is going to be, on average, only a little more religious than a male Ph.D. But a woman who has a high school education will be quite a bit more religious than a man who has a high school education.

## Employment Status

Baylor University sociologist Rodney Stark developed a theory that men are less religious than women because men evolved to be risk takers. Men roamed about, taking risks as the species evolved — hunting and gathering and facing external evils to attain goals and adapt to the environment. These risk-taking men, the theory goes, could not afford to worry about the future. If they did, they wouldn't take risks anymore. Nature having suppressed their capacity to worry about risk, men need not be as religious because they didn't need its help in reducing worry. Women had no such need to avoid thinking about risk. Therefore, these less risk-taking women were (and are) more inclined to want the security that religious beliefs bring. Some researchers have looked directly at attitudes about risk and have found gender differences that help support this theory.

I am not sure if this theory allows us to speculate about risk taking and religion today, but it's worth looking at. Meg Whitman, now CEO of Hewlett-Packard, should be less religious than a woman her age who is sitting at home. Lady Gaga, identified by *Forbes* as earning $90 million a year, should be less religious than a woman her age who is not in the workforce. These extreme examples highlight the general idea that as a woman who is employed moves into more of a risk-taking mode (working, being evaluated, having to cope with the pressures of a job, and so forth), she has to force herself not to worry about the consequences of her risky situation. Therefore, she has less need for religion's risk-avoidance benefits. Or more simply, an employed woman might have more of a sense of control over her life, or more power, or less need to worry, depending on her job and income. An employed woman would thus be less religious than a woman who is not employed.

The accompanying chart displays importance of religion by employment and gender *by age*. The patterns are fascinating.

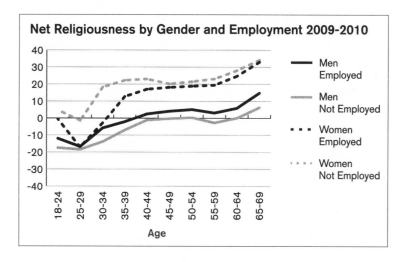

At every age, women who are not employed *are* more religious than women who are employed.

Among men, the opposite pattern prevails. *Employed* men are more religious at all ages than nonemployed men. *This certainly suggests that the functions of religion are different for women than for men.* And it gives some support to the idea that women may be more religious than men because of their employment status. Religion may work as a support mechanism for women who are fulfilling traditional roles in society, but women who are fulfilling less traditional roles (i.e., employed) may not need religion as much.

One caveat. The workforce participation rate of women has increased dramatically over the last 50 years in the U.S. This would suggest that the religious gender gap should have shrunk concomitantly. It has not, as far as we can tell.

## Marriage

A functionalist approach could argue that married women are closer to performing their integrative role in society than unmarried women. Marriage is also the precursor to child rearing, which in turn could activate more integrative thoughts among women, including religion. So, married women should be more religious than unmarried women. And marital status should make no difference among men.

A conflict theory approach might argue that married women seek religion as a refuge from their less powerful state that comes with a traditional marriage. Women who are not married have, in effect, more power. Men, with a different historical role in the marriage relationship, would have the same religious consciousness whether they are married or not.

Let's turn to the data. Our mission: to see if marital status affects the religious intensity of women more than it affects the religious intensity of men.

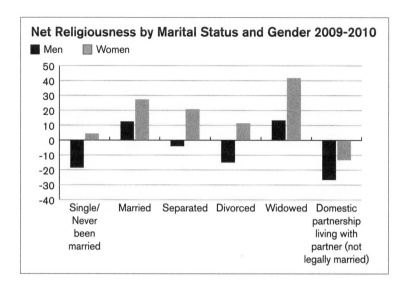

The results clearly show that the gender gap exists in *all* marital status groups. *Men are as affected by marital status as women.*

Among singles, women have higher average levels of religiousness than men. This occurs despite the fact that women who are single and never married presumably have not experienced either the "oppression" of marriage or the activation of the integrative instinct that marriage brings about.

Women who live with a domestic partner are much less religious than women in all other marital statuses. Yet men living with domestic partners are *even less* religious. Women who are widowed are more religious than women in any other marital status. They "out-religion" widowers as well. And so forth across every other marital status. The gender gap persists, relentlessly, without regard for the marital status of the individual.

We did a multivariate statistical analysis that yielded the same findings. The gender gap in religiousness persists after controlling for marital status (and also controlling for age, education, children in the home, race, region of country, and party identification).

Marital status relates to religion. But it does so for men just as much as it does for women. We don't find much help in explaining the gender gap by looking at marital status. Getting married, or having been married, does little to change the differences in religiosity between men and women.

---

### Bottom Line

Women are more religious than men in the U.S. This finding goes back to the beginning of modern survey research. Some historical research suggests that women were more religious than men long before that. A review of the results from a comprehensive survey of religion in countries around the world shows that women also appear to be more religious than men in the significant majority of the world's countries.

I am amazed at the persistence of the religious gender gap across almost every segment of society. Age, marital status, religious orientation, income, children — all for the most part don't seem to affect the fact that women are just basically more religious than men. Women, surprisingly, are already more religious than men at age 18. And, at age 80 and older, women are still more religious than men.

It simply may be that women are hardwired to be more religious than men, reflecting some evolutionary advantages that this provides for our species. That's very difficult to prove. The data I reviewed in this chapter suggest that women are more religious than men at least in part because of their historically more dependent position in society. Women who have lower levels of education and who are not employed are more religious relative to men at the same socio-economic positions and at the same ages. But these differences get smaller among women who have more education and who are employed.

All of these patterns are subject to change in the years ahead, to some degree depending on the overall shape of the economy. Women's participation in the labor force rose steadily through the last half of the 20th century. By 2010, the civilian labor force participation rate among women was 62%, up from 38% in 1960. But the growth in the percentage of women working has leveled off and become stable in recent years.

Gallup data show no signs that young women today are more likely to be working — compared with men — than older women. In fact, among young Americans, the gap between the percentage of women and men who work is larger than the gap among older men and women. As today's middle-aged and older women die off, it does not appear that the younger women replacing them will be more inclined to work relative to men. It's possible, although by no means certain, that we could actually see an *increase* in religiousness in the general population in the years ahead if women become less likely to be employed.

Women with higher levels of education are less religious than those with lower levels of education — at all ages. If women continue to gain on the education front, we could see a *decrease* in religiousness across the population. The government tells us that an increasing percentage of women in fact do have college degrees compared with men. Gallup data show the same thing. Younger women are more likely than men to have college degrees. At about age 55, that pattern flips; among older Americans, men are the most likely to be college educated. If these patterns keep up, the overall percentage of women with college degrees should therefore increase as older, less well-educated women die off. This could lower the average religiousness of the population.

The culture and structure of gender differences in society will no doubt change in many other ways in the future. All of these changes could affect the relative pattern of religiousness of men and women in the years ahead. Regardless of the *potential* effect of these changes, it's important to reiterate that so far, there has been no decrease in the net religiousness of women compared with men among younger Americans, at least that we can detect. Eighteen-year-old women today are more religious than 18-year-old men, just as they have been for decades.

We would expect that higher religiousness among women would result in more females in church leadership roles as the social barriers to women's participation in many professions continue to fall. It would not be surprising to find the majority of clergy in the future to be women, at least in some faiths. Based on the data, a scenario in which female clergy lead worship services filled with a majority of women could become reality. That is what's happening in some churches.

Increasing numbers of female ministers are finding their way into the pulpits in Episcopalian, Presbyterian, and Methodist churches. As a result, the clergy in these and other mainline

Protestant denominations is becoming more of a "pink collar" profession. Famous evangelical ministries are incorporating women in highly prominent ways. The huge nondenominational Lakewood Church in Houston lists Victoria Osteen as "co-pastor" of the church along with her husband, Joel, and features several other women as key parts of its ministries team. The famous Crystal Cathedral in Orange County, California, was founded by Dr. Robert Schuller, but after inner turmoil, began to list his daughter Sheila Schuller Coleman as Executive Director of Ministry and Mission, although the Crystal Cathedral ministry was forced to sell the church in 2010.

The anomalous situation, of course, comes from those religious traditions that continue to prohibit women from being ministers, priests, or rabbis. These include most significantly the two largest religious bodies in the United States — the Roman Catholic Church and the Southern Baptist Convention — along with a number of fundamentalist religious groups. These structural patterns are based on interpretations of scripture and history by those in charge of these groups. But these traditions fly in the face of what appears to be a fundamental truth — women are more religious than men. It remains to be seen how long these patterns can persist in these large denominations. Many women remain loyal Catholics and Southern Baptists, of course. But will they in the future?

The "femaleness" of religion in the U.S. could accelerate as part of a self-fulfilling prophecy. If women increasingly occupy positions of religious leadership, the entire religious enterprise could become more female-centric. This could expand the gender gap in religion in the years to come.

# CHAPTER VIII

## Religion Is a Class Act

In the language of sociologists, religion in America is *socially stratified*, with significantly different average levels of education and income across the religious spectrum.

This should not be surprising. Americans across all aspects of life do what comes naturally — group themselves according to their social status. Many religious groups originated precisely to satisfy the needs of certain market segments. Other religious groups modified their theologies and practices over the years to appeal to certain groups of people. Americans tend to self-select into religions and denominations that are congruent with their other statuses.

Jews and Episcopalians are at the top of America's economic heap, enjoying average income and education levels well above all other religions. Religiously conservative evangelicals — Baptists, Pentecostals, Assemblies of God members — are at the bottom of the economic spectrum. Catholics — the largest single religious group in America today, comprising almost one-fourth of all Americans — are generally in the socio-economic middle.

This system of religious stratification may change. Economic inequality in the United States is increasing rather than decreasing. Economically upscale Americans tend to use religion not so much for its personal benefits or functions, but on a relative basis more for its social functions. Rich Americans may find it more important than ever to worship in a socially distinct religious group. Health-conscious upscale Americans may also figure out that religion provides wellbeing benefits and become more interested in religion as a result.

Americans at the bottom of the economic ladder are more likely than their rich cousins to be religious because it is important to them personally. If economic woes continue to disproportionately affect the middle and lower classes, they may increasingly seek religions that speak to their depressed situations. Religious leaders may focus more on the needs of these less fortunate people. In an economically unstable state, religion may also take on more of an activist edge for those at the bottom of the social hierarchy — a classic social justice positioning for religion. We could witness a shift in middle-class and lower-class theology from providing relief from sorrow to providing remedies for sorrow. The clergy could be leading the "Occupy" movements of the future.

At the same time, as we saw in Chapter II, undifferentiated, unaffiliated religions and nondenominational churches are growing, along with the number of Americans with no explicit religious identity. This could lead to a blurring of status distinctions, particularly among the young, as bigger churches with a bigger socio-economic tent attract more of all types of parishioners.

## STATUS GROUPING OF RELIGIONS

Americans group themselves with others of similar status in terms of neighborhood living patterns, club memberships, vacation destinations, recreational activities, entertainment and dining out, choices of cars, hair and dress styles — and even patterns of speech.

It should be no great shock to find that Americans tend to practice this same pattern of status grouping in the realm of religion. Many religious groups in America, particularly smaller ones, are composed of adherents with distinct socio-economic profiles.

Just 2% of Americans are Jewish. But Jews are the most upscale religious group in the country. Sixteen percent of Jews say they have a high school education or less, while 37% say they have a postgraduate degree, the latter higher than any other religious groups in the U.S. Jews have the highest incomes of any of major religious group we measure at Gallup. Almost one-third of American Jews report incomes of $90,000 a year or more — twice the national average.

Mormons and those who affiliate with non-Christian religions — also smaller slices of the American religious pie — are more likely to be college graduates than are Protestants or Catholics.

Slightly more than half of Americans are Protestants, and nearly one-fourth of Americans are Catholics. Taken as a whole, Protestants and Catholics are similar on socio-economic measures. This is mainly a result of the huge size of these groups. They cannot mathematically deviate too much from the overall average because they *define* the average. But, and this is the fascinating point, Protestants can subdivide and subdivide into smaller and smaller groups, and it's these groups that provide us with much more status-distinct segments.

There are literally hundreds if not thousands of brands of Protestants. About a dozen or so of these brands are what I would call the major Protestant groups. But beyond these groups are hundreds of additional denominations, many too small to be analyzed. And today we have a growing number of Protestant groups that are unbranded and unaffiliated with any pre-existing denomination. These smaller religious groupings are much more capable of developing distinctive socio-economic patterns. The smaller the group, the easier it is for that group to deviate from the average. (That's why, of course, it's hard for mutual fund managers to maintain above-average performance when their successful funds grow huge).

The large number of relatively small Protestant denominations gives rise to a distinctly American phenomenon of significant importance — religious switching. The U.S. religious system is highly porous, making it easy to move from one religious group to another. Protestant denominations and groups, by definition, share the same large umbrella of non-Catholic Christianity. They share doctrinal and religious behavior similarities. Shifting one's identity and membership among these groups is relatively painless. Protestants thus have the opportunity to select their religious identity to match their socio-economic status. Protestants can choose religious denominations that align with their education and income — a process of assortative mating. This helps sustain the socio-economic grouping of denominations.

Individual Protestant denominations range widely up and down the socio-economic spectrum. Just 16% of Pentecostals have college degrees. That compares with 57% of Episcopalians with college degrees. Fifty-two percent of Pentecostals have no college education compared with 21% among Presbyterians and Episcopalians. Mainline denominations associated with aristocratic America stand out at the top of the educational spectrum. Baptists and Pentecostals are at the other end, based on their relative lack of formal education.

Education and income are positively correlated. We are not surprised to find the same denominational hierarchies in relationship to income that we found in relationship to education. Episcopalians are the richest Protestant denomination. Pentecostals and Baptists are among the poorest.

We have already seen that non-Christian groups, including in particular Jews, have above-average socio-economic status. To this group we can add Episcopalians, Presbyterians, and other mainline Protestant groups. These are the socio-economic elite of America's religious structure.

These patterns of religious stratification are well-established. Sociologist James Davidson ranked religions based on median household income, education, and — interestingly — representation among members of Congress. On this basis, he concluded that Episcopalians, Jews, Presbyterians, and Unitarian Universalists constitute the nation's "upper-stratum" on the status hierarchy. Members of the Church of Christ, Seventh-Day Adventists, Assembly of God, Baptists, Muslims, Church of God, and Jehovah's Witnesses are at the low end of the spectrum.

An analysis by the Pew Forum on Religion & Public Life showed much the same pattern, with the addition of some small religious groups like Hindu, Orthodox, and Buddhist into the top status groups of religions.

Episcopalians have historically been disproportionately represented among U.S. presidents, reinforcing the idea of a religious elite in this country. (Although to some extent, this reflects the prevalence of the Episcopalian religion, or its close relatives, in the early years of the republic). Despite their high socio-economic status, there have been no Jewish presidents, which reflects a different social pattern in the U.S. Mitt Romney, the 2012 Republican candidate for president, is a Mormon — none of whom have served as president. Catholics make up about a quarter of all Americans but have had only one of their number serve as president. As befits the current move to unbranded religions, President Barack Obama is a general Protestant who worships at different types of churches, when he goes, in Washington, D.C. His predecessor, George W. Bush, was raised in the Episcopalian and Presbyterian traditions but took up the Methodism of his wife Laura. And Bill Clinton was a Southern Baptist by heritage. To date, there has not been a president who publicly declared that he had no religion. In fact, more than four in 10 Americans say they would not vote for an atheist for president — but that again is another story.

## EXPLANATIONS

We humans have a strong instinct to be part of the "in crowd," no matter how we define it. People choose communities, neighborhoods, and streets within communities based on the social characteristics of the people who live there. Kids strive desperately to be accepted into the correct social grouping. So do many of their parents.

People who attain higher levels of income and education arrange their lives so they can associate with people of similar high socio-economic status and avoid associating with people of lesser socio-economic status. Well-off people generally like to make it publicly known through various means of status differentiation that they possess superior social positioning. An upper-class woman's choice of hair style, clothes, jewelry, automobile, leisure-time activities, vacations, and private schools for her children all let the world, or the part of the world in which she is interested, know she is upper-class.

Americans who are highly status-conscious can sniff out the socio-economic status of a gathering, institution, or group within seconds — preening positively if it is high, perhaps making a quick exit if it is low. A person of a "lower class" may pay little attention to how you grasp your fork; an "upper-class" person can be intensely focused on how you handle your silverware as an important indicator of your relative status and breeding. A person of a certain lower class may be oblivious to the fabric and tailoring of your $2,000 dress; an upper-class matron will be instantly aware of the garment's cost and will grant you the status it provides accordingly.

This type of socio-economic differentiation pervades much of our existence. Differences in income, education, and other measures of social prestige determine life chances, affect people's life choices, and are related to almost every aspect of an individual's life. The results? Americans occupy positions in the social structure that carry with them a number of linked and consistent statuses. The upper classes have different ZIP codes, retail shopping preferences, lifestyles, clothing choices, tastes in entertainment, automobiles, and vacation venues than the lower classes. People of different socio-economic status talk differently from one another, eat differently, have different preferences in food, and are interested in different recreational pursuits.

Religion is part of this process. The tentacles of the American class octopus stretch deep inside the nation's religious system. Not all Episcopalians have Ph.D.s, M.D.s, or law degrees. Not all Pentecostals drop out of school after the eighth grade. There are poor Episcopalians, and there are rich Pentecostals. Some Southern Baptist churches, primarily located in big Southern cities, have congregations who are well-to-do and who represent the city's elite. But we are dealing here with averages. And the average differences in socio-economic status across religions are clear. A visitor from Mars stumbling into a Jewish synagogue or an Episcopalian worship service is more likely to come face to face with wealthy people than if that same visitor drops into a Pentecostal or Baptist church.

Religious scholars have been studying the link between religion and socio-economic differentiation for many years. Certain non-Catholic Christian denominations clearly arose in the first place to meet the needs of specific social class groups. In the pre-Civil War era, blacks needed a religion that fit their subjugated status. A religion that emphasized that one's success here on earth is an indication of preordained entry into heaven — as did Calvinism — would not have fit well with the life situation of black slaves. A religion emphasizing that what happens here on earth does not matter and that puts emphasis on the afterlife was a much better fit. This was the Baptist church, which took root among blacks.

Methodism prospered in the U.S. partly because it fit the needs of farmers and poor people in the 18th and 19th centuries. The Episcopalian denomination was imported from England by the original Anglo settlers of the U.S. As "old families" with ties to the Revolution gained social status, so did their religion.

Denominations continue to shift and transform to adapt to changing needs of population segments — just as is the case for any other business. In a situation with many religious groups competing for members, market forces take over. Religious groups cater to market segments, often distinguished by socio-economic status.

Remember Robin Williams' character Vladimir Ivanoff in the movie *Moscow on the Hudson*? Young Vladimir, who hailed from Cold War Russia, found himself flummoxed by the virtual cornucopia of things to buy in America's Bloomingdales. Well, Americans today can find themselves, at least in theory, equally dumbfounded by the cornucopia of religions they can choose from. The vast number of religious groupings in the U.S., and the fact that many of these religious groupings are highly similar, provide a great marketplace of religions from which members of the population can select. Americans can and do "shop" their religion.

A recent study by the Pew Forum on Religion & Public Life found that more than four in 10 respondents say they have switched religions: "More than one-quarter of American adults (28%) have left the faith in which they were raised in favor of another religion — or no religion at all. If change in affiliation from one type of Protestantism to another is included, 44% of adults have either switched religious affiliation, moved from being unaffiliated with any religion to being affiliated with a particular faith, or dropped any connection to a specific religious tradition altogether."

This whole pattern of religious switching is a fascinating phenomenon. I wrote a scholarly review of religious switching some years back in an article published in the *American Sociological Review*. As I discussed then, there are many reasons for religious switching. One reason for switching is the desire to shop denominations to fit with changing life situations. People who are socially mobile, particularly upwardly mobile, make changes to reflect their new statuses. Not only do newly rich people buy a fancy car, invest in expensive clothes, move to a super-rich ZIP code, and join the right country club, but they also may switch religions. The wide umbrella of Protestant denominations makes this quite easy. Baptists who get rich become Episcopalians. An Episcopalian who falls on hard times can become a Baptist. Class mobility can lead to religious mobility.

This system of religious mobility could be a reason why the U.S. is so much more religious than other developed countries around the world. In Spain, for example, most people are Catholic. If one is unhappy with being a Catholic, the only choice is to leave the Catholic church and thus leave religion altogether. In the U.S., if one is raised Catholic and becomes unhappy with Catholicism, one can select among hundreds of other Christian religions and denominations or unaffiliated, nondenominational churches — rather than abandoning the whole religious enterprise. The uniquely American ability to invent or reinvent religious groups as needed most certainly helps keep religion vibrant in this country.

## SOCIAL CLASS AND INDIVIDUAL RELIGIOUSNESS

A famous verse from Mathew 19:23-24 in the New Testament states: "And Jesus said to his disciples, 'Truly, I say to you, only with difficulty will a rich person enter the kingdom of heaven. And again I tell you, it is easier for a camel to go through the eye of a needle than for a rich person to enter the kingdom of God.'" Jesus also said: "If you would to be perfect, go, sell what you possess and give to the poor, and you will have treasure in heaven; and come, follow me."

The "eye of the needle" verse has generated much thought over the years. Some biblical scholars argue that the authors did not mean that the eye of the needle in question was a sewing needle (which would be very difficult indeed to go through), but rather a gate outside Jerusalem. Others say that the word *camel* was mistranslated and should be *rope*. Whatever the precise meaning, the concept appears to be straightforward: Religion and wealth do not necessarily mix well.

This premise has been taken to heart by priests, nuns, monks, and other clerics who take vows of poverty. Many religions take as part of their doctrine, at least superficially, the idea that the focus in life should not be on things or acquiring possessions.

Not everyone agrees. Joel Osteen is a Houston, Texas, evangelist whose church is so large that it holds services in a former NBA basketball arena. Osteen's television broadcasts reach millions of worshipers — fittingly, since he began his career as a producer for his evangelist father's television broadcasts. Osteen believes that not only can religion and wealth coexist, but that religion can and should lead to financial reward. No eye of the needle for Pastor Osteen! He declares, "Remember, God delights in your prosperity! He wants to do something supernatural and new in your finances, even now! But it's up to each one of us to perceive it and know it. You do that with your faith! No one else can do that for you. Receive God's Word into your spirit by agreeing with God, and then you can expect God to move in your finances!"

Other preachers and evangelists in the U.S. have joined Osteen over the years in focusing on the so-called "prosperity gospel," arguing that rather than running from wealth, religious people should embrace it.

Obviously, theologians and preachers have embraced a number of ways of looking at the relationship between religiousness and socio-economic success. Likewise, many social scientists and other thinkers have pondered how religion fits into a society's class structure.

Karl Marx was one thinker who had strong ideas about religion. He believed that people at the bottom of the heap, the proletariat, used religion for specific reasons. Or rather, religion was forced on them for specific reasons. As Marx famously put it: "Religion is the sigh of the oppressed creature, the heart of a heartless world, and the soul of soulless conditions. It is the opium of the people." Marx thought that the oppressed needed religion to help them deal with their "heartless" world and their "soulless" conditions.

Marx argued that the ruling class (the owners of means of production) also used religion for specific reasons — namely, to keep the proletariat in place. Religion was a means to calm the masses, a way of defusing angst about the wretched circumstances of the present with a promise of the heavenly rewards of the future. Marx dismissed anyone who was religious as having a false consciousness that had not yet been liberated. This is in some ways similar to the views of the "New Atheists," who argue that religious humans' consciousness is deluded.

Another famous scholar who looked into these matters was Max Weber, a German sociologist who contributed a variety of approaches to the discipline of sociology over his life (1864-1920). One of Weber's famous works was *The Protestant Ethic and the "Spirit" of Capitalism*. Weber argued that capitalism arose in the West in part because the Protestant religion helped people abandon their traditional view of the world and focus on decisions and rational action. Weber focused on Calvinism in particular. He pointed out that under Calvinism, acquiring wealth became a sign of being a member of the predestined elect or anointed and therefore legitimated working hard and acquiring value. That in turn was consistent with capitalism.

Weber's thesis in the years since *The Protestant Ethic and the "Spirit" of Capitalism* was published has been harshly criticized. Some claim it is not supported by available evidence. Note that Weber was talking about the "rise" of capitalism. This gives pause to those who now note that capitalism has risen in countries like Japan, South Korea, China, and Taiwan. None of these countries has a religious heritage based on Protestantism. The spirit of capitalism can obviously arise without the spur of the Protestant ethic.

For our purposes here, the salient point about Weber's work is his general idea, as was the case with Marx, that religious beliefs and practices have economic consequences.

## THE WELL-TO-DO USE RELIGION DIFFERENTLY

Let's turn to the data relating to the connection between education, income, and individual religiousness. Our first conclusion: Those at the top of the socio-economic spectrum score lowest on our overall scale of religiousness.

The differences in religiousness across socio-economic levels persist even when we control statistically for various factors including age, region of country, and gender.

The basic measure of net religiousness I'm using in this book has two components: self-reported importance of religion and church attendance. In this instance, I want to look at these separately. It turns out that each has a different type of effect on religiousness — a very important finding.

Self-reported importance of religion decreases as education increases. If you have a postgraduate degree, you are about 10 points less likely to say religion is important in your life than if you have a high school degree or less. Church attendance, however, is a different animal. Americans with the highest levels of education attend religious services just as often as those with lower levels of education. No matter how well-educated you are, you still attend church with about the same frequency as those with lower levels of education.

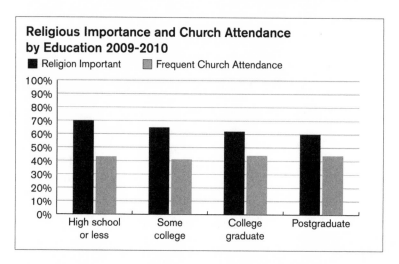

Importance of religion and church attendance are highly correlated with one another and typically relate to other variables in the same way. But religion provides an exception. Intrinsic, personal aspects of religion appear to function differently than the external, public, outward behavioral aspects of religion when it comes to social class.

We find the same patterns in relationship to income. Church attendance is pretty flat across income categories, peaking a little in the middle income ranges. Those with the highest levels of income go to church just as often as those with the lowest levels of income. But, importance of religion drops significantly as income increases.

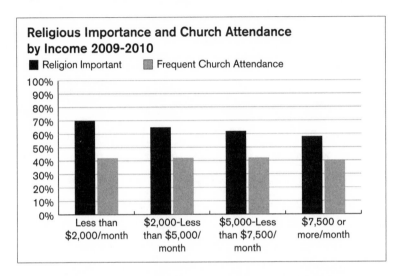

It is clear that Americans with lower levels of education and income disproportionately value the personal aspects of religion. At the same time, these Americans do not put any more value on the social aspects of religion (religious service attendance) than do those with higher levels of education and income. Why would this be?

## MANIFEST AND LATENT FUNCTIONS OF RELIGION

As I write this, large groups of protestors are occupying parts of New York City; Washington, D.C.; Boston; and other cities as part of the Occupy Wall Street movement. The *manifest* functions of these protests are to express outrage and anger at various grievances relating to big business' power and income and wealth inequality. The *latent* or less obvious functions of these protests are to provide personal meaning to the individual protestors, many of whom are young, perhaps unemployed, relatively anomic, and unmoored by conventional social structures. Being part of a movement gives these people meaning and purpose, instant social networks and friends, and an accepting cultural milieu.

Students in high school like to join groups and organizations. The *manifest* functions of membership in these groups are fairly clear. A high school math club meets to help students explore math. The French club meets to bring students together who are learning French. But as any smart young high school student will tell you, there's more to it than that. Joining a club has many *latent* or less obvious functions. It is a way to meet other people and to butter up the teacher who sponsors the club. And, of course, many students have figured out that joining clubs can help bolster their résumé and, they hope, enhance their chances of getting into selective colleges.

So, if we did a sociological analysis of a high school math club, we would discover that the benefits of student participation were in many instances far removed from math per se. These benefits — meeting people, impressing faculty, boosting one's college acceptance chances — are the latent functions of club membership.

Upscale Americans, as we have seen, use the communal, churchgoing aspects of religion just as much as those who are not so well-off — even though the former are personally less religious. No doubt, upscale Americans worship in a public setting for the same straightforward, *manifest* reasons as anyone else. Worshippers express their personal beliefs in the company of many others. They join together with others of a like faith community, worship God communally, share religious experiences, jointly hear religious instruction, work as a group to help others or to evangelize and convert, experience joy together, sing together, and help out on other religious projects. Worshipers of all socio-economic strata reap the general togetherness that comes from a common religion doctrine and ritual.

But upscale Americans may disproportionately value *latent* benefits from church attendance — compared with those who have lower levels of education and income. These benefits are not explicitly part of what the religion was set up to do. Latent functions can be unconscious and even unintended, but powerful nevertheless.

Church participation fulfills a basic human need for social affiliation — being together with other people. Humans are, after all, social animals bred through evolution to live and die in and through a series of social groups. Going to church puts one in the presence of others, working with others, sitting side by side with others. An extension of this benefit is social networking. Participating in religious social groupings provides people with the opportunity to meet friends, potential customers, babysitters, and community "influentials." Religious ritual participation also provides substantial opportunities for cementing social ties, publicly displaying membership in certain social strata, and in general demonstrating one's place in the local social hierarchy. And, as we have seen, church attendance may provide wellbeing and health benefits.

If you are successful and upscale, the theory goes, you may have less need for the personal benefits of religion. Upscale Americans may develop alternative philosophic systems that help guide them through life. Rich people have the means to consult personal psychiatrists and to use other mental help support systems. They have more connections to nonreligious organizations and groups that provide peace of mind. And most importantly, better educated and higher income Americans may have less to worry about in a material sense and therefore need the personal benefits of religion less. In short, they may not need the manifest or obvious benefits of church attendance as much as those who are less well-off. But, and this is the crucial point, they may value and need the latent, social, communal aspects of religion more — and that's what keeps them going to church. Lower income Americans presumably cling to religion like a lifeboat, using it as consolation from sorrow and in many ways as an antidote to their daily misery and challenges.

All in all, it is clear that upscale and downscale Americans relate to religion in different ways. Religion is more *personally* important to Americans with lower levels of education and income. Religion appears to be proportionately more *socially* important to Americans with higher educations and higher incomes, in part because of the latent benefits it provides.

All of this provides an important insight into understanding religion in this country. Americans tend to use religion and religious expression in different ways that reflect their position in the American social system.

## A NOTE ABOUT PRAYER AND BELIEF

Religious practices such as prayer mimic the pattern we found with *personal* importance of religion. Data from the NORC General Social Survey for 2000 to 2008 show that 62% of those with less than a high school education say they pray at least once a day. That compares with 49% of those with graduate degrees.

Gallup asked about prayer and belief in God in a May 2010 survey. Respondents were given three choices: There is a God who answers prayers, there is a God but one who does not answer prayers, or there is no God.

Answers to this question are clearly related to education and income. Belief in a God who answers prayers drops from 92% among those who have a high school education or less down to 71% among those with postgraduate degrees. Similarly, 90% of those with low incomes say there is a God who answers prayers, compared with 78% of those making $90,000 a year or more.

Those with higher levels of education (and to a lesser degree, higher levels of income) are less likely to say there is a God who answers prayers and more likely to say that there is a God but that this God does not answer prayers — or no God at all. This underscores the less personal nature of religion for those at the top of the socio-economic scale.

---

## Bottom Line

Religion is highly intertwined with the socio-economic system in this country and always has been. Two sociologists, James D. Davidson and Ralph E. Pyle, recently wrote a book called *Ranking Faiths: Religious Stratification in America* in which they declare: "Religious stratification has always been and continues to be an important part of our society."

The relationship between religion and class, as we have seen, has two parts. First, religious *groups* in America have markedly different socio-economic profiles. Second, *individual* Americans seem to use religion differently in their daily lives based on their socio-economic status.

Looking ahead, what types of changes in these relationships might we see in the coming years? Economic forces are fundamental components of human social life and social structure. The search for scarce resources defines the nature of the evolutionary process by which species develop, change, and survive. These forces are highly connected with religion. If the nature of religion changes in society, that could affect the economic structure of society. And if economic structures change, that will affect religion.

Social critics have been emphasizing the looming possibility of increasing economic turmoil in the years ahead, perhaps coupled with an increase in income inequality as the rich get richer and the rest of society stagnates or gets worse. When a society enters this type of economic shaky period, social institutions and cultural patterns adjust accordingly. Religion is no exception. If we do have more economic instability and richer rich people coupled with more and more poor people, Americans may begin to respond to religion differently. And, sensing an opportunity, religious groups may begin to emphasize issues that relate to the deteriorating socio-economic status of their followers.

As we have seen in this chapter, religion provides many functions for its adherents. Religious denominations (and specific churches and pastors within them) often establish doctrinal emphases that fit the needs of their parishioners. Few Episcopalian ministers with wealthy congregations are going to preach Sunday after Sunday that people should relinquish their possessions and join the ranks of the poor. Few Pentecostal ministers are going to preach that being rich is a sign that one has been anointed by God.

Some critics think that religion blinds workers to the unjust structure of inequality in social systems. They think that workers should therefore throw off religion in an attempt to enhance their class consciousness and recognition of stark reality. That's certainly one way to go, but there are other possibilities. Workers and those at the bottom of the socio-economic system can *use* religion as a philosophic and theological basis for fighting back at the system.

Again, religion can provide several functions for those with lower levels of education and income. One such function is the traditional "surcease for sorrow" benefit that comes from acknowledging God's love and the possibility of a better tomorrow in the afterlife. But another function religion can play for the downtrodden or oppressed is more radical — using religion as the justification for actions to change and overturn societal structures, systems, and cultural patterns. Religious groups with more economically troubled members could in theory turn in this direction.

This would not be a new phenomenon. Catholic priests in this country and particularly in Latin American countries have long protested unjust economic systems in the name of religious principles. The Social Gospel movement in the U.S. fought against perceived economic injustices based on the principles of the New Testament. President Obama himself raised this possibility in a prayer breakfast speech he made in February 2012, when he in essence said that the principles of Christianity call for more care and concern for the lower classes.

Thus, a key development to watch in the years ahead will be how religious organizations react to the economic changes besetting American society. Religious groups may well begin to insert themselves more actively into the political system, helping channel their members' economic angst into political or social action.

We certainly noticed in February 2012 that the Catholic hierarchy in the U.S. got highly involved in the political process. Catholic bishops reacted against the provision of the 2010 Affordable Care Act that required Catholic hospitals, schools, and agencies to provide birth control as part of their insurance policies. This, the bishops said, violated Catholic principles. The Catholic hierarchy publicly protested, sent sermons around for local parish priests to read at Sunday Mass, and in general brought enough pressure to bear that the Obama administration ultimately had to react — in part by modifying its policies. In short, a religious group was attempting to change or affect government policy on this issue.

This was fairly safe ground for Catholic bishops. It was not a challenge to the fundamental structure of society. The Catholic hierarchy was not protesting the rising ranks of the unemployed in the U.S., the increase in home foreclosures, rising income inequality in general, or the basic economic structure of our society. But it's possible that a more radical shift in focus to more fundamental issues could come in the future.

We know that conservative evangelical groups have been involved in politics for decades. Again, they have been focused more on social and values issues than on economic or broad political issues. But, this appears to be changing, as I will discuss in Chapter IX.

Facing economic deprivation, the poor may start looking for religions that provide a justification for changing the system. And religious leaders may comply. The Occupy Wall Street movement has not had an overtly religious component. But it is possible that in the future, such demonstrations will be led by firebrand priests and preachers, rallying their flocks in the name of religion to protest and change what they perceive to be the nation's unjust economic system.

It's by no means certain that American society will become more unequal in the years ahead, with increasing income inequality and more grouping of society into the rich and the not rich. But if it does, we could also see more assortative religious grouping. The rich generally attempt to differentiate themselves from the rest of society. In a society in upheaval, the rich may more aggressively seek religious groups that cater to their needs and that are populated by fellow rich people.

As we have seen, people at the upper end of the socio-economic spectrum are, on a relative basis, more likely to use religion for its social aspects than value it for its personal importance. And upscale Americans are apparently more sensitive to health-related issues, given that they have lower rates of smoking and obesity. It is thus possible that these upscale Americans will increasingly put the two together — recognizing the payoff that church attendance could have for their personal wellbeing. If so, they are likely to seek out religious togetherness with people of the same social class. This could fuel a renaissance in membership and activity for denominations associated with Americans who have higher incomes and higher levels of education.

There are other currents at work that can affect the relationship between religion and the country's status system in the years ahead. These include the expansion of nonbranded religion, both at the individual and congregational level. The whole system of religious stratification could become *less* of a factor in the future if this general drift in religious and denominational identification in America continues. Undifferentiated, less formal, nondenominational religious groupings may have less of a sense of socio-economic identity than long-standing denominations and be more open to worshippers who have diverse social status. This could lead to a homogenization of religion in this country, perhaps leaving the shrinking mainline Christian denominations with a smaller, but increasingly isolated, upscale constituency.

One thing is clear. Changes in the relationship between religion and class will be an important element of the evolution of our society and culture in the years ahead.

# CHAPTER IX

## The Potential for a More Direct
## Influence of Religion

James Surowiecki, in his book *The Wisdom of Crowds*, talks about the influence of the Quakers in British society during the 18th and 19th centuries. These Quakers didn't overtly attempt to change their society or convert people to their religion. Quaker businesspeople were simply honest and reliable in their dealings. But as an indirect result, they transformed how business was conducted between Britain and America.

Sociologist Max Weber argued that the Protestant ethic in Europe led to the development of capitalism. It wasn't that Europeans set out to use their religion directly and overtly to develop a new economic system. The religious system had an indirect effect on the ability of capitalism to flourish, or so Weber argued.

Certainly, having a neighborhood full of religious people can affect the neighborhood — even if those religious people are not explicitly propagating their faith. Imagine if your neighborhood consisted mostly of evangelical Christians, Mormons, devout Muslims, or Catholic nuns. Or, imagine that everyone in your neighborhood had no formal religious identity. In any of these cases, your neighborhood would likely be markedly different than it is today.

The degree of religiousness in a society affects its culture. Highly religious people are more likely to be married and less likely to live in domestic partnerships. Highly religious Americans are also more likely to say that gay and lesbian relationships are morally unacceptable, to oppose abortions and stem cell research, and to say that having a child out of wedlock is unacceptable. Nonreligious Americans are less in favor of restrictions on matters relating to marriage and reproduction.

The major institutions that operate in any social system — legal, educational, family, economic, political, and religious — are intertwined with and affect one another. Religion is one of the most influential of these systems. Religious people can have an effect on the society they live in *just by being there.*

This idea fits into the sociological assumption that religion performs a number of functions in society. Religion provides meanings, explanations, and buttressing for a society, or elements of that society, as it progresses. Sociologist Peter Berger called this the "sacred canopy" that overarches a social system and culture to support and legitimate the arrangements therein.

Every social group, organization, or society needs to have certain functions fulfilled to survive. One such function is maintaining cohesion and integration of the members so that everyone is not fighting everyone else. Another is maintaining social stability so that the society and its members can ease through the transition points in life — births, deaths, marriages, and so forth. Religion helps perform these functions. As Berger argued, religion's sacred canopy gives these things a sense of correctness, legality, and reason for being.

The religious factor in American society makes the society profoundly different than it would be if there were no religion. A social system is an extremely complex bunch of moving parts. Societies collapse, change, and cease to function. The presence of religion helps these moving parts keep going in demonstrably distinct ways.

The fact that religion may allow society to function more smoothly with minimal disruptions is a good thing, as long as one assumes that how society exists is better than how it could exist if it were disrupted. Critics — as I have discussed in previous chapters — often focus mainly on this latter point. They argue that if a society is arranged in an unjust and unfair way, religion performs the negative function of legitimating an illegitimate system. Radicals throughout history have argued that disruption in social systems is good, helping shake things up and paving the way toward the final utopian society. This, of course, rarely works as planned. But the bottom line is the bottom line: Religion has a profound *indirect* effect on the society and culture in which it resides, for better or worse, as we have seen throughout this book.

## ATTEMPTS TO CHANGE SOCIETY DIRECTLY IN THE NAME OF RELIGION

We may, in the years ahead, see increasingly more *direct* effects of religion that result from attempts to change society in the name of religion. These effects may be profound, in part because religion provides in essence a very strong justification for making changes.

Religion inculcates in the hearts and souls of its true believers the power of doing things in the name of God, the divine, the sacred. This makes religion potentially an extremely important factor in today's contemporary societies — both in the U.S. and around the world. The suicide attacks of Sept. 11, 2001, in New York City and Washington, D.C., show what humans are capable of doing when they believe — or are led to believe — that they are acting in the name of their religious beliefs.

Attempting to change society in the name of religion is not new. Religious groups have throughout history taken steps to specifically and directly change and affect the society, culture, and people around them. This goes back to the great founders of religion. They and those who came immediately after them encouraged their followers to proselytize and convert others.

The New Testament is full of stories of Jesus' attempts to alter the way people around him lived their lives and went about their daily activities. It was in the name of religion that thousands of Crusaders set out in the 11th, 12th, and 13th centuries to change the lives of people living in the Holy Lands. Many other wars and political actions have occurred over the centuries in the cause of or sanctioned by religion. Americans have shot and killed doctors who perform abortions, and more than 2,500 people were killed on Sept. 11 — all in the name of religion.

Changing society in the name of religion is a dramatic shift from the perspective that religion should be distinct from society. It's also a shift from the perspective that the main influence of religion on society should be the indirect process of converting others to its beliefs.

I was told as a young man growing up as a Southern Baptist in Texas that converting others to Christianity (the Southern Baptist variety specifically) was a central mission of our religion. My father, a Southern Baptist minister and theologian, used to preach at revivals. The success of those revivals was measured by the number of people who "walked the aisle" — that is, got up from their chairs at the end of the service to the accompaniment of rousing hymns, walked to the front of the sanctuary, and announced to the minister that they were converting to Christ. I attended many of these revivals myself. In between revivals, Baptists used to pray for the souls of those not yet converted to Christ.

My grandfather was also a Baptist leader, and he spent his life attempting to bring religion to the lives of young people, particularly college students. He had heart disease late in his life. According to his biographer, my grandfather asked his friends to pray for him to live so that he could continue to influence young people's lives. My grandfather didn't spend the last years of his life trying to change laws, promote new legislation, or in any other way directly affect society. He was content with the less confrontational approach of bringing the word of his religion to others.

This has changed. Southern Baptists have become more outwardly focused. The Ethics & Religious Liberty Commission (ERLC), an arm of the Southern Baptist Convention, was created to address issues relating to the society in which Baptists live. In recent years, the ERLC has become quite activist in its efforts to influence and change aspects of society deemed to stand in contradiction to Southern Baptist principles. The ERLC's longtime president, Richard Land, was heavily involved in taking positions on social issues and appearing as a conservative commentator across the media until his retirement in 2012.

Southern Baptists still engage in personal evangelism, to be sure. But Southern Baptists now feel it's appropriate to get involved with and take positions on the issues of the day. Baptists, along with others, have decided to break out of the bounds of personal religion and a focus on conversion. Baptists now make a determined effort to influence and change laws, policies, and politicians in the greater society around them.

Evangelism, in short, has to some degree become passé. Conversion of individuals is not enough. Increasingly, religious Americans are attempting to change how people live their lives and to change social institutions, laws, and policies using whatever means are available, including the electoral and political process.

There is of course a history of these types of society-changing efforts. I mentioned the Crusades, the centuries-long push in the name of religion to go forth and bring control of the Middle East back into Christian hands. More recently (and far less dramatically), we have the example of the Woman's Christian Temperance Union (WCTU), a group that has always fascinated me. WCTU members made it their business to not only avoid drinking alcohol themselves, but to change society so that it was illegal for *anyone* to drink alcohol. The WCTU, with "Christian" in its very name, helped push for passage of the 18th Amendment, which took effect in 1920 and banned the sale of alcohol in the U.S. (The 18th Amendment of course was wildly unsuccessful, underscoring the difficulty inherent in the attempt to change society in the name of religious beliefs.)

The WCTU was also involved in attempts to fix social problems and societal ills among the poor and exploited in society.

It is hard to quantify exact changes over time in how religion has been used as the justification for attempts to transform cultures and societies. But the attempt to change society in the name of religion does appear more prominent now than in the recent past. In February 2012, Republican presidential candidate Rick Santorum announced as much when he declared that he "almost threw up" after reading John F. Kennedy's 1960 campaign speech. That's the speech in which Kennedy came down firmly for a separation of church and state. Santorum declared, "The idea that the church can have no influence or no involvement in the operation of the state is absolutely antithetical to the objectives and vision of our country." The implications — for the U.S. and the world — of this religious justification for action will be more and more apparent in the years to come.

## RELIGIOUS AND NONRELIGIOUS AMERICANS HAVE DIFFERENT WORLDVIEWS

In the broadest sense, American society today is sharply divided by religion. Not in the sense of religious *identity* as in Catholic-Protestant differences in Northern Ireland or Muslim-Hindu disputes in India and Pakistan. But in terms of the division of America into groups of those who are religious and those who are nonreligious. This religious division spills out in general views about culture and society. These views in turn have a significant effect on the political reality of society.

Beginning with the Carter administration, and in particular in the Reagan years, we became aware of the "religious right." In other words, *religious* Americans connected with *right* (i.e., conservative) causes.

Thus, the divide in American society between those who are religious and those who are not is wed, at least partially, to the divide in American politics between those on the right and those on the left. Highly religious Americans have a higher probability of being Republicans (black Americans are a special case in contemporary politics because they are overwhelmingly religious and Democrats). Less religious Americans have a higher probability of being independents or Democrats. This is one of the most significant patterns in American politics today.

Religious Americans bring to the Republican Party their belief in the legitimacy of traditional structures and structured traditions. Religious people tend to approach life in the context of religious tenets, laws, rules, beliefs, and norms. This translates into a belief in the value of preserving marriage structures, status hierarchies, inequalities, and other traditional patterns of society. Religious individuals embrace the idea that patterns in society exist for a reason. Therefore, existing social realities have rationales — values, as it were — that undergird and explain them. This was highly religious Republican candidate Santorum's position in the 2012 presidential election.

Nonreligious Americans, naturally enough, have less of this sense of the ultimate meaning or rationale for the way things are. Lacking a sense of the religious "canopy" that stretches over society and helps legitimate and explain why things are what they are, less religious Americans are more likely to, in essence, proclaim that anything and everything in a social system is up for grabs. Without religion as a buttress or legitimating force, these Americans are free to call into question existing or potential cultural norms. Social arrangements and norms have no particular inherent justifications. Everything is open.

This plays out fairly obviously in terms of social norms and structures built around reproduction. Religious Americans (who tend to be Republicans) believe in a legitimated rationale for ordered, normatively controlled systems governing family and sexual relations. Nonreligious Americans (who tend to be independents and Democrats) tend to see no one arrangement or pattern of sexual (family) relationships as more justifiable than any other. Thus we have Republicans endorsing, as one example, traditional approaches to marriage as being only between a man and a woman. Democrats endorse, as an example, the right of individuals of the same gender to choose marriage.

The divide between the religious and the nonreligious can extend further into societal arrangements — beyond these family-values focus points. For the nonreligious, the idea that there is no legitimating religious force in play means that there is less of an inherent rationale for *anything* in society. This includes systems that result in inequalities, one of the defining social issues of our time. Thus, the political party that represents the less religious (the Democratic Party) is more likely to advocate changes, ameliorations, modifications, and control of society's systems for distributing power, income, and wealth (i.e., pushing for equality). The political party that represents the more religious (the Republican Party) is more inclined to advocate and live with the status quo, implicitly assuming that it exists for a reason.

We have a religiously based, legitimated system on the one hand and a system that essentially has less of a basis for structures or norms on the other. We have two different directions: The religious-based Republicans focus on preservation and acceptance of the status quo. The more nonreligious Democrats focus on change and remedies.

## Bottom Line

The religion and religiosity of the citizens of a country have an indirect effect on many aspects of the country in which they live. Beyond this, religious citizens often attempt to change the society around them by converting others to their religion. And, more dramatically, highly religious citizens can attempt to change fundamental aspects of society in the name of religion. We may well see more of this type of change in the years ahead.

In the political realm, Republicans have most actively embraced religion and used religious beliefs as the basis for their views of social and political policy. Democrats have been less involved. But the Democratic Party may attempt to change this divide in the years ahead. In line with the general trend by which religion will be increasingly used as the basis for attempts to change society, Democrats may start using religion as the foundation for their perspective on societal arrangements. We saw the beginnings of this with President Obama's prayer breakfast speech in February 2012.

These types of efforts may attract more religious people to the Democratic Party. If so, we could have the spectacle of dueling religious parties in the years ahead, both arguing that their interpretation of religion justifies their views of how society should be arranged and run. Any party that embraces religious Americans has the advantage of the emotion and motivation that comes with religious beliefs. Nothing is as motivating as a belief that what one is doing is based on a higher calling or response to divine initiative. This gives those who mobilize religious Americans a significant advantage in efforts to modify the society they see around them.

# CHAPTER X

## Summing it Up: The Future of Religion

As should be clear by this point, religion is fundamentally intertwined with many aspects of American society. The nature of this dynamic relationship has continually evolved since the country's inception. It's clear that it will continue to change in the years ahead. And in many ways, it's possible that religion will be more, rather than less, significant.

### THE AGING OF THE POPULATION

Americans in their 60s, 70s, and 80s today are substantially more religious than those who are younger. The size of these senior age groups is set to expand dramatically as baby boomers grow older over the next two decades. It is likely that these aging baby boomers will adopt the religiousness of their elders, albeit possibly in different forms. There is evidence that this is already occurring. Should this trend continue, an already widely religious America will become even more so. New Atheism notwithstanding, we may in fact be on the cusp of a religious renaissance.

There is some question about the future religiousness of the nation's younger generation. Marriage and childbearing are both associated with religiousness. The U.S. is currently experiencing lower rates of marriage, higher rates of living in domestic partnerships, and a lowered fertility rate. These trends could affect overall religiousness in the future, although there is little sign of it to date.

## RECOGNITION OF THE BENEFITS OF RELIGION

Religious people have higher wellbeing, better emotional health, and in some instances better physical health than those who are not religious. This well-documented correlation between religiousness and wellbeing will likely become more widely acknowledged, leading almost certainly to expanded efforts to understand the underlying processes involved. This understanding will lead to methods for taking advantage of the processes to help reach societal wellbeing and health objectives.

Americans, particularly baby boomers, will increasingly look for ways to maintain or expand their wellbeing and happiness in future years. They may increasingly seek out religion as part of that quest. Additionally, government and businesses may recognize the benefits of religion for lowering healthcare costs and take direct and indirect steps to reward those who prove they are religious.

## THE UNBRANDING OF RELIGION

Americans increasingly say that they do not have a specific religious identity. And Americans who do have a religious identity increasingly use broad terms like "Christian" to define it rather than naming a specific group. At the same time, other indicators of religiousness are remaining fairly stable. We are thus witnessing a shift in how Americans express their religiousness as much as or more than an actual decrease in their religiousness per se.

More and more Americans identify with and worship in unbranded, nondenominational contexts. Membership in classic, traditional, standard churches is declining.

This drop in membership in mainline Protestant denominations is related to low birth rates, the lack of new Protestant immigrants, loss of members as they age, failure to convert, and the transference of their members to nondenominational churches. Thus, traditional mainline churches' numbers will shrink even as nondenominational churches down the street continue to grow.

Numbers-wise, the Catholic church will continue to be rescued by the high fertility rates of religious young Hispanics, even as its non-Hispanic members leave. And the Catholic church will edge closer and closer to becoming a majority Hispanic church in the years ahead. The Catholic church is almost 30% Hispanic already today, and almost half of younger Catholics are Hispanic.

## AN INCREASED EMPHASIS ON THE COMMUNITY ASPECT OF RELIGION

The religion of tomorrow may increasingly emphasize informal aspects of community and less hierarchy. Growth will come to branded churches to the extent that they emulate nondenominational approaches and highlight community, togetherness, and social fabric ties. Religious leaders will recognize that the social lives of today's potential parishioners are more and more involved with ad hoc groupings, informal networking, and interaction with those who share affinities. Americans will increasingly recognize that the social and community aspects of religion are very valuable.

## A CHANGE IN THE RELATIONSHIP BETWEEN RELIGION AND SOCIO-ECONOMIC STATUS

Higher personal religiousness is associated with lower positioning on the socio-economic ladder. A decrease in economic stability in this country could potentially increase restlessness, dissatisfaction, and perhaps anger among those in the lower socio-economic rungs of society. Religions may respond to socio-economic disruption by helping assuage the pain of deprivation. Or religions may respond by invoking a social justice position — involving religions more directly in the attempt to change society to help the disadvantaged, up to and including encouraging protest and political action.

The socio-economic division of religion in American society could thus expand as economic inequality expands. The more advantaged class, which uses religion more for its social aspects, may increasingly isolate itself into very class-specific religions. Members of the less advantaged class may find solidarity in religions that address their socio-economic deprivations.

At the same time, the proliferating numbers of large nondenominational churches could become melting pots for Americans of all socio-economic positions in society.

## FEMALIZATION OF RELIGION AND THE SQUEEZE OUT OF MALE-CENTRIC RELIGIONS

Women are more religious than men. This is a universal fact across age, religion, ethnicity, and geographic location — in the U.S. and in the majority of countries around the world. There could be some shrinking of this gender gap in the U.S. if more women become better educated and more likely to work in the years ahead.

The role of women in religion is already changing. The percentage of women in the ranks of the clergy in mainstream Protestant faiths is rapidly increasing. This fits with women's higher religiousness. At the same time, women are prohibited from the clergy in Catholic and conservative Protestant faiths. This may cause increasing tension in these faiths in the years ahead as their most religious members chafe at finding themselves unable to participate in church leadership. Catholic and fundamentalist Christian faiths could find themselves in a gender crisis, either losing female adherents or having to change their male-dominant structures in a bow to the reality of the social culture and systems in which they operate.

## POLITICS

Religion in America today is intertwined with politics. Although highly religious blacks are overwhelmingly Democrats, highly religious white Americans are more likely to be Republicans than those who are less religious. Consequently, the white segment of the Democratic Party today is composed of Americans for whom religion is less important and who attend church less frequently. Religion also has a major influence *within* the Republican Party. Highly religious Protestant Republicans push for socially conservative candidates who espouse strict allegiance to strong family-values principles and pull back from candidates who are more moderate.

The Republican Party's monopoly on the loyalty of religious white Protestants has given it a highly motivated core of voters. This has in turn had a profound effect on American politics. That could change. President Barack Obama's prayer breakfast speech in February 2012 showed evidence that the Democratic Party is increasingly aware of its weak positioning among religious Americans. The GOP has structured its appeal to religious voters based on family values and moral issues. The Democrats may increasingly emphasize their positions on justice, equality, and compassion as justifications for a connection between being religious and being a Democrat. Religious Americans may become the next major partisan battleground in American politics.

## THE INCREASE IN HISPANICS AS A PROPORTION OF THE U.S. POPULATION

Hispanics are more religious than the average American. Even with a lowered Hispanic immigration rate, the percentage of Hispanics within the U.S. borders will increase in the years ahead. This is a result of internal reproduction — many babies from the young Hispanic population already in this country because of the recent, massive in-migration of Hispanics. The increase in mostly Catholic Hispanics in the U.S. will help sustain the Catholic church and will help keep the religiousness of the U.S. higher on average in the years ahead.

## AMERICANS' MIGRATION TO MORE CULTURALLY RELIGIOUS STATES

The 50 states of the union have distinct cultures that affect their politics and their religion. This occurs despite the massification of America resulting from shared media, mass marketing, and mobility. A state's culture of religion persists for the most part despite the composition of religions within its borders or other demographic factors. Those who live in Mississippi are vastly more religious than those who live in Vermont. This difference in religious culture helps make these two states substantially different places. We see some signs that states with the most religious cultures are expanding in population at a greater rate than states with a less religious culture. This could lead to an overall increase in religiousness in the years ahead.

---

### Bottom Line: Where We Are Headed

There are two broad alternative paths for the future of religion in America. The United States could follow the secularization path of many European countries. Or America could continue to blaze its own religious trail with religion changing, morphing, and transmuting itself into new but still vibrant forms. The evidence in this book points to the latter — an America that will become a more religious nation in the years ahead, albeit one that may look a lot different, religiously speaking, than it does today.

# REFERENCES

Much of the analysis in this book is based on aggregated interviews with representative samples of the U.S. adult population collected as part of the Gallup-Healthways Well-Being Index tracking project. This unprecedented project involves interviews with samples of 1,000 randomly selected national adults each night. Complete details on the methodology of this ongoing project are available at http://www.well-beingindex.com/methodology.asp.

A large part of the analysis in this book involves the aggregate of 706,691 interviews conducted in 2009-2010. At times, the analyses use data aggregates involving other dates. Additionally, some data in the book derive from the traditional U.S. population surveys Gallup has been conducting going back to the 1940s. In all instances, the dates and source of the data are noted in the text.

Other sources and related references are listed here alphabetically by chapter.

## INTRODUCTION: RELIGION IS THE ELEPHANT IN THE ROOM

Adherents.com. (2005). *Largest religious groups in the United States of America*. Retrieved August 22, 2012, from http://www.adherents.com/rel_USA.html

Dawkins, R. (2006). *The God delusion*. Boston: Houghton Mifflin Harcourt.

Gallup, G. H., Jr. (2002, December 17). *Why are women more religious?* Retrieved August 22, 2012, from http://www.gallup.com/ poll/7432/why-women-more-religious.aspx

Gallup, G. H., Jr. (2003, July 29). *War changed prayer habits of many Americans.* Retrieved August 22, 2012, from http://www.gallup. com/poll/8944/war-changed-prayer-habits-many-americans.aspx

Grimes, W. (2011, December 16). Christopher Hitchens, polemicist who slashed all, freely, dies at 62. *The New York Times.* Retrieved August 22, 2012, from http://www.nytimes.com/2011/12/16/arts/ christopher-hitchens-is-dead-at-62-obituary.html?pagewanted=all

Hamilton, B. E., Martin, J. A., & Sutton, P. D. (2003). Births: Preliminary data for 2002. *National Vital Statistics Reports, 51*(11). National Center for Health Statistics. Retrieved August 22, 2012, from http://www.cdc.gov/nchs/data/nvsr/nvsr51/nvsr51_11.pdf

Mather, M., & Lavery, D. (2010, September). *In U.S., proportion married at lowest recorded levels.* Retrieved August 22, 2012, from the Population Reference Bureau website: http://www.prb.org/ Articles/2010/usmarriagedecline.aspx

Miner, H. (1956). Body ritual among the Nacirema. *American Anthropologist, 58*(3), 503-507.

Newport, F. (2010, May 21). *In U.S., increasing number have no religious identity.* Retrieved August 22, 2012, from http://www.gallup.com/ poll/128276/increasing-number-no-religious-identity.aspx

Newport, F. (2010, June 25). *Americans' church attendance inches up in 2010.* Retrieved August 22, 2012, from http://www.gallup.com/ poll/141044/Americans-Church-Attendance-Inches-2010.aspx

Newport, F. (2010, December 29). *Near-record high see religion losing influence in America.* Retrieved August 22, 2012, from http:// www.gallup.com/poll/145409/near-record-high-religion-losing-influence-america.aspx

Newport, F. (2011, June 3). *More than 9 in 10 Americans continue to believe in God.* Retrieved August 22, 2012, from http://www.gallup.com/poll/147887/americans-continue-believe-god.aspx

Newport, F. (2011, July 1). *Religion and party ID strongly linked among whites, not blacks.* Retrieved August 22, 2012, from http://www.gallup.com/poll/148361/Religion-Party-Strongly-Linked-Among-Whites-Not-Blacks.aspx

Newport, F. (2012, March 27). *Mississippi is most religious U.S. state.* Retrieved August 22, 2012, from http://www.gallup.com/poll/153479/Mississippi-Religious-State.aspx

Newport, F., Agrawal, S., & Witters, D. (2010, December 1). *Very religious Americans report less depression, worry.* Retrieved August 22, 2012, from http://www.gallup.com/poll/144980/Religious-Americans-Report-Less-Depression-Worry.aspx

Newport, F., Agrawal, S., & Witters, D. (2010, December 23). *Very religious Americans lead healthier lives.* Retrieved August 22, 2012, from http://www.gallup.com/poll/145379/Religious-Americans-Lead-Healthier-Lives.aspx

Newport, F., Witters, D., & Agrawal, S. (2012, February 16). *Religious Americans enjoy higher wellbeing.* Retrieved August 22, 2012, from http://www.gallup.com/poll/152723/religious-americans-enjoy-higher-wellbeing.aspx

Sam Harris website. (n.d.). http://www.samharris.org

Slack, G. (2005, April 30). The atheist. *Salon.* Retrieved August 22, 2012, from http://www.salon.com/2005/04/30/dawkins/

Smith, R. S. (1995). Giving credit where credit is due: Dorothy Swaine Thomas and the "Thomas Theorem." *The American Sociologist, 26*(4), 9-28.

TED. (n.d.). *Richard Dawkins: Evolutionary biologist.* Retrieved
August 22, 2012, from http://www.ted.com/speakers/richard_
dawkins.html

## CHAPTER I: IN GOD WE STILL TRUST

Finke, R., & Stark, R. (1993). *The churching of America, 1776-1990:
Winners and losers in our religious economy.* New Brunswick, NJ:
Rutgers University Press.

Finke, R., & Stark, R. (2005). *The churching of America, 1776-2005:
Winners and losers in our religious economy.* New Brunswick, NJ:
Rutgers University Press.

Lim, C., MacGregor, C. A., & Putnam, R. D. (2010). Secular and
liminal: Discovering heterogeneity among religious nones. *Journal
for the Scientific Study of Religion, 49*(4), 596-618.

Newport, F. (2011, June 3). *More than 9 in 10 Americans continue to
believe in God.* Retrieved August 22, 2012, from http://www.gallup.
com/poll/147887/americans-continue-believe-god.aspx

The Pew Forum on Religion & Public Life. (2009). *Faith in flux:
Changes in religious affiliation in the U.S.* Retrieved August 31, 2012,
from http://www.pewforum.org/uploadedfiles/Topics/Religious_
Affiliation/fullreport.pdf

Saad, L. (2011, June 20). *In U.S., 22% are hesitant to support a Mormon
in 2012.* Retrieved August 22, 2012, from http://www.gallup.com/
poll/148100/Hesitant-Support-Mormon-2012.aspx

Stark, R. (2008) *What Americans really believe.* Waco, TX: Baylor
University Press.

*Three Great Awakenings in America.* (n.d.) Retrieved August 31, 2012,
from http://www.sermonindex.net/images/3greatawakenings.pdf

## CHAPTER II: AMERICA REMAINS A CHRISTIAN NATION, BUT DIFFERENT NOW

AFP. (2008, February 25). *Protestants on verge of becoming minority in US: study.* Retrieved August 23, 2012, from http://afp.google.com/article/ALeqM5h7rc3tC9fKhoJW6X9PV6ZmG2BIng

All About Baptists website. (n.d.). http://www.allaboutbaptists.com/groups.html

Armstrong, D., Dave1988, et al. How many Protestant denominations are there? (2005, April 12). Message posted to http://www.philvaz.com/apologetics/a120.htm

The Associated Press. (2008, May 9). Hispanic growth fueled by higher fertility rates. *Daily News.* Retrieved August 23, 2012, from http://www.nydailynews.com/latino/hispanic-growth-fueled-higher-fertility-rates-article-1.329145

Catholics, Mormons, Assemblies of God growing; mainline churches report a continuing decline. (2010, February 12). National Council of Churches. Retrieved August 24, 2012, from http://www.ncccusa.org/news/100204yearbook2010.html

Chilton, J. B. (2007, November 5). *Demography and time trends in membership in the Episcopal Church.* Retrieved August 23, 2012, from http://www.episcopalcafe.com/daily/evangelism/diagnosing_mainline_decline.php

Dinnerstein, L., & Reimers, D. M. (1999). *Ethnic Americans: A history of immigration* (4th ed.). New York: Columbia University Press.

An ethical Mormon life. (2009, October 8). *BBC.* Retrieved August 29, 2012, from http://www.bbc.co.uk/religion/religions/mormon/socialvalues/ethics_1.shtml

Johnson, B. R. (2011, January 20). *The good news about evangelicalism: Evangelicalism isn't shrinking and the young are not becoming liberals.* Institute for Studies of Religion, Baylor University. Retrieved August 23, 2012, from http://www.baylorisr.org/2011/01/first-things-the-good-news-about-evangelicalism/

Kerby, R. (n.d.). *Have Americans lost faith in the old "mainline" churches?* Retrieved August 23, 2012, from http://www.beliefnet.com/Faiths/Home-Page-News-and-Views/Have-Americans-lost-faith-in-the-old-mainline-churches.aspx

Kessler, G. (2012, February 17). The claim that 98 percent of Catholic women use contraception: a media foul. *The Washington Post.* Retrieved August 23, 2012, from http://www.washingtonpost.com/blogs/fact-checker/post/the-claim-that-98-percent-of-catholic-women-use-contraception-a-media-foul/2012/02/16/gIQAkPeqIR_blog.html

Kosmin, B. A., & Keysar, A. (2009). *American religious identification survey (ARIS 2008).* Trinity College. Retrieved September 5, 2012, from http://commons.trincoll.edu/aris/files/2011/08/ARIS_Report_2008.pdf

Lindner, E. W. (Ed.). (2005). *Yearbook of American & Canadian churches 2005: Whither global mission?* Nashville, TN: Abingdon Press.

Migration Policy Institute. (n.d.). *US historical immigration trends.* Retrieved August 22, 2012, from http://www.migrationinformation.org/datahub/historicaltrends.cfm

*Muslim Americans: A national portrait.* (2009). The Muslim West Facts Project. Retrieved August 30, 2012, from http://www.gallup.com/se/ms/153572/REPORT-Muslim-Americans-National-Portrait.aspx

Newport, F. (1979). The religious switcher in the United States. *American Sociological Review, 44,* 528-552.

Newport, F. (2012, May 22). *Americans, including Catholics, say birth control is morally OK*. Retrieved August 23, 2012, from http://www. gallup.com/poll/154799/Americans-Including-Catholics-Say-Birth-Control-Morally.aspx

Official denominational web sites. (n.d.). Hartford Institute for Religion Research. Retrieved August 24, 2012, from http://hirr. hartsem.edu/denom/homepages.html

The Pew Forum on Religion & Public Life. (2009). *Faith in flux: Changes in religious affiliation in the U.S.* Retrieved August 31, 2012, from http://www.pewforum.org/uploadedfiles/Topics/Religious_Affiliation/fullreport.pdf

Pew Research Center. (2011, July 14). *The Mexican-American boom: Births overtake immigration*. Retrieved August 23, 2012, from http://www.pewhispanic.org/2011/07/14/the-mexican-american-boom-brbirths-overtake-immigration/

Saad, L. (2006, March 17). *Attitudes toward family size among Palestinians and Israelis*. Retrieved August 23, 2012, from http://www.gallup.com/poll/21940/Attitudes-Toward-Family-Size-Among-Palestinians-Israelis.aspx

Smith, T. W., & Kim, S. (2004). *The vanishing Protestant majority* (GSS Social Change Report No. 49). NORC/University of Chicago. Retrieved August 22, 2012, from http://www-news.uchicago.edu/releases/04/040720.protestant.pdf

Thumma, S. (1996). *Exploring the megachurch phenomena: Their characteristics and cultural context*. Hartford Institute for Religion Research. Retrieved August 23, 2012, from http://hirr.hartsem.edu/bookshelf/thumma_article2.html

Van Marter, J. L. (2012, January 26). Evangelical Covenant Order unveils polity. *Presbyterian News Service*. Retrieved August 23, 2012, from http://www.pcusa.org/news/2012/1/26/evangelical-covenant-order-unveils-polity/

Westbury, J. (2008, May 22). Have Southern Baptists joined the evangelical decline? *The Christian Index*. Retrieved August 23, 2012, from http://www.christianindex.org/4421.article

Williamson, T. (2009, October-November). Cooperative Baptist Fellowship — liberal Baptists in action. *The Fundamentalist Digest*. Retrieved August 24, 2012, from http://www.fundamentalbaptistministries.com/Archives/ COOPERATIVE%20BAPTIST%20FELLOWSHIP.htm

## CHAPTER III: RELIGION IS GOOD FOR YOUR HEALTH

The Advisory Board Company. (2012, February 17). *Going for gold: Cleveland Clinic saves by boosting worker wellness*. Retrieved August 23, 2012, from http://www.advisory.com/Daily-Briefing/2012/02/17/Cleveland-Clinic-employee-wellness

Blue, L. (2010, July 28). Recipe for longevity: No smoking, lots of friends. *Time*. Retrieved August 23, 2012, from http://www.time.com/time/health/article/0,8599,2006938,00.html

Centers for Disease Control and Prevention. (2011). *Tobacco-related mortality*. Retrieved August 23, 2012, from http://www.cdc.gov/tobacco/data_statistics/fact_sheets/health_effects/tobacco_related_mortality/

Centers for Disease Control and Prevention. (2012). *Economic facts about U.S. tobacco production and use*. Retrieved August 23, 2012, from http://www.cdc.gov/tobacco/data_statistics/fact_sheets/economics/econ_facts/

Childs, E. (2010). Religious attendance and happiness: Examining gaps in the current literature—a research note. *Journal for the Scientific Study of Religion, 49*(3), 550-560.

Cleveland Clinic. (n.d.). *Who we are and what we do*. About Wellness Institute. Retrieved August 23, 2012, from http://my.clevelandclinic.org/wellness/aboutus.aspx

Crabtree, S. (2010, April 28). *Income, education levels combine to predict health problems.* Retrieved August 23, 2012, from http://www. gallup.com/poll/127532/Income-Education-Levels-Combine-Predict-Health-Problems.aspx

The Daniel Plan website. (n.d.). http://www.danielplan.com/

Deaton, A. S. (2009). *Aging, religion, and health* (NBER working paper no. 15271). National Bureau of Economic Research. Retrieved August 23, 2012, from http://www.nber.org/papers/w15271.pdf

Framingham Heart Study website. (2012). http://www. framinghamheartstudy.org/

Gallup. (2012, February 16). *The links between religion, wellbeing, and health.* [Video of Gallup event]. Washington, D.C.: Gallup World Headquarters. Retrieved August 23, 2012, from http:// www.gallup.com/video/152798/Gallup-Event-Religion-Wellbeing-Health-Part.aspx (Part 1) and http://www.gallup.com/ video/152801/Gallup-Event-Religion-Wellbeing-Health-Part. aspx (Part 2).

Gillum, R. F., King, D. E., Obisesan, T. O., & Koenig, H. G. (2008). Frequency of attendance at religious services and mortality in a U.S. national cohort. *Annals of Epidemiology, 18*(2), 124-129.

Goszkowski, R. (2008, March 21). *Among Americans, smoking decreases as income increases.* Retrieved August 23, 2012, from http://www. gallup.com/poll/105550/Among-Americans-Smoking-Decreases-Income-Increases.aspx

Holt-Lunstad, J., Smith, T. B., & Layton, J. B. (2010). Social relationships and mortality risk: A meta-analytic review. *PLoS Medicine, 7*(7). Retrieved August 23, 2012, from http://www. plosmedicine.org/article/info%3Adoi%2F10.1371%2Fjournal. pmed.1000316

Lim, C., & Putnam, R. D. (2010). Religion, social networks, and life satisfaction. *American Sociological Review, 75(6),* 914-933.

Mendes, E. (2011, November 17). *Smoking rates remain highest in Kentucky, lowest in Utah.* Retrieved August 23, 2012, from http://www.gallup.com/poll/150779/smoking-rates-remain-highest-kentucky-lowest-utah.aspx

National Episcopal Health Ministries website. (2009). http://www.episcopalhealthministries.org/about-health-ministry

National Institute of Mental Health. (n.d.). *Major depressive disorder among adults.* Retrieved August 23, 2012, from http://www.nimh.nih.gov/statistics/1mdd_adult.shtml

Newport, F., Agrawal, S., & Witters, D. (2010, December 1). *Very religious Americans report less depression, worry.* Retrieved August 22, 2012, from http://www.gallup.com/poll/144980/Religious-Americans-Report-Less-Depression-Worry.aspx

Newport, F., Witters, D., & Agrawal, S. (2012, February 16). *Religious Americans enjoy higher wellbeing.* Retrieved August 23, 2012, from http://www.gallup.com/poll/152723/religious-americans-enjoy-higher-wellbeing.aspx

*Norman Vincent Peale (1898-1993): Champion of positive thinking.* (n.d.). Retrieved August 23, 2012, from http://normanvincentpeale.wwwhubs.com/

Park, M. (2012, January 24). Rick Warren and church tackle obesity. *CNN.* Retrieved August 23, 2012, from http://www.cnn.com/2012/01/24/health/saddleback-warren-diet/index.html

Peale, N. V. (1952). *The power of positive thinking.* New York: Ballantine Books.

Peterson, C., & Seligman, M. E. P. (2004). *Character strengths and virtues: A handbook and classification.* New York: Oxford University Press.

Saad, L. (2012, August 22). *One in five U.S. adults smoke, tied for all-time low.* Retrieved August 23, 2012, from http://www.gallup.com/poll/156833/one-five-adults-smoke-tied-time-low.aspx

Vecsey, G. (1993, December 26). Norman Vincent Peale, preacher of gospel optimism, dies at 95. *The New York Times.* Retrieved August 29, 2012, from http://www.nytimes.com/1993/12/26/obituaries/norman-vincent-peale-preacher-of-gospel-optimism-dies-at-95.html?pagewanted=all&src=pm

Witters, D. (2012, January 20). *Key chronic diseases decline in U.S.* Retrieved August 23, 2012, from http://www.gallup.com/poll/152108/Key-Chronic-Diseases-Decline.aspx

## CHAPTER IV: RELIGION AND POLITICS

Adherents.com. (2006). *Religious affiliation of U.S. presidents.* Retrieved August 24, 2012, from http://www.adherents.com/adh_presidents.html

Ballot measures: California Proposition 8: Ban on gay marriage. CNN Election Center 2008 exit polls. *CNN.* Retrieved August 24, 2012, from http://www.cnn.com/ELECTION/2008/results/polls/#val=CAI01p1

The Barna Group. (2007, January 18). *Survey explores who qualifies as an evangelical.* Retrieved August 24, 2012, from http://www.barna.org/barna-update/article/13-culture/111-survey-explores-who-qualifies-as-an-evangelical

Bingham, A. (2012, January 17). The 'moderate' skeletons in Mitt Romney's past. *ABC News.* Retrieved August 24, 2012, from http://abcnews.go.com/Politics/OTUS/moderate-skeletons-mitt-romneys-past/story?id=15373893#.T7lZJfldn8c

Civil rights movement. (n.d.). Retrieved August 24, 2012, from the John F. Kennedy Presidential Library and Museum website: http://www.jfklibrary.org/JFK/JFK-in-History/Civil-Rights-Movement.aspx

Dart, J. (1987, November 7). Evangelical impact on U.S. society: Theologians use varying yardsticks. *Los Angeles Times.* Retrieved August 24, 2012, from http://articles.latimes.com/1987-11-07/local/me-4839_1_evangelical-movement

Desegregation of the armed forces: chronology. (n.d.). Retrieved August 24, 2012, from the Harry S. Truman Library & Museum website: http://www.trumanlibrary.org/whistlestop/study_collections/desegregation/large/index.php?action=chronology

Gallup. (2012). U.S. presidential election center. [Interactive data application]. http://www.gallup.com/poll/154559/US-Presidential-Election-Center.aspx?ref=interactive

Hughes, S. (2012, February 26). Santorum: 'I almost threw up' after reading JFK speech on church, state. *The Wall Street Journal.* Retrieved August 24, 2012, from http://blogs.wsj.com/washwire/2012/02/26/santorum-i-almost-threw-up-after-reading-jfk-speech-on-church-state/

Katz-Hyman, M. B., & Rice, K. S. (2011). *World of a slave.* Santa Barbara, CA: ABC-CLIO.

Layman, G. C., & Hussey, L. S. (2005, December). *George W. Bush and the evangelicals: Religious commitment and partisan change among evangelical Protestants, 1960-2004.* Paper presented at the University of Notre Dame conference on "A Matter of Faith? Religion in the 2004 Election," Notre Dame, IN.

Lee, C. E. (2012, February 2). Obama makes religious case for his economic policies. *The Wall Street Journal.* Retrieved August 24, 2012, from http://blogs.wsj.com/washwire/2012/02/02/obama-makes-religious-case-for-his-economic-policies/

Matthews, T. (n.d.). *The religion of the slaves.* Retrieved August 24, 2012, from http://www.mamiwata.com/slavery1.html

Moyers, B. (2006). *Is God green? Religion and politics.* Retrieved August 24, 2012, from http://www.pbs.org/moyers/moyersonamerica/print/religionandpoliticsclass_print.html

Newport, F. (2006, March 16). *Protestants and frequent churchgoers most supportive of Iraq war.* Retrieved August 24, 2012, from http://www.gallup.com/poll/21937/protestants-frequent-churchgoers-most-supportive-iraq-war.aspx

Newport, F. (2009, June 12). *Women more likely to be Democrats, regardless of age.* Retrieved August 24, 2012, from http://www.gallup.com/poll/120839/women-likely-democrats-regardless-age.aspx

Newport, F. (2012, April 25). *Religiousness a key factor for Romney and Obama support.* Retrieved August 23, 2012, from http://www.gallup.com/poll/154097/Religiousness-Key-Factor-Romney-Obama-Support.aspx

Oppenheimer, M. (2012, May 25). A campaign pitch rekindles the question: Just what is liberation theology? *The New York Times.* Retrieved August 24, 2012, from http://www.nytimes.com/2012/05/26/us/a-campaign-pitch-rekindles-questions-about-liberation-theology.html?ref=politics

The Pew Forum on Religion & Public Life. (2009, February 10). *A look at religious voters in the 2008 election.* Retrieved August 24, 2012, from http://pewresearch.org/pubs/1112/religion-vote-2008-election

Primary resources: New Deal a square deal for the negro? [Editorial by Jesse O. Thomas, *Opportunity: Journal of a Negro Life,* October 1933]. Retrieved August 29, 2012, from PBS website: http://www.pbs.org/wgbh/americanexperience/features/primary-resources/fdr-square-deal/

Rick Santorum wins supermajority support from Texas meeting of conservative leaders. (2012, January 14). *PR Newswire.* Retrieved August 24, 2012, from http://www.prnewswire.com/news-releases/rick-santorum-wins-supermajority-support-from-texas-meeting-of-conservative-leaders-137363088.html

Roberts, C., & Inskeep, S. (2004, July 2). Lyndon Johnson's fight for civil rights. *NPR.* Retrieved August 24, 2012, from http://www.npr.org/templates/story/story.php?storyId=3087021

Rothenberg, S., & Newport, F. (1984). *The evangelical voter: religion and politics in America.* Washington, D.C.: Free Congress Research & Education Foundation.

Santorum wins key southern states in strong challenge to Romney. (2012, March 14). *Public Radio International.* Retrieved August 24, 2012, from http://www.pri.org/stories/politics-society/santorum-wins-key-southern-states-in-strong-challenge-to-romney-8915.html

Stanley, P. (2012, January 4). Evangelical leaders plan Texas meeting to discuss possible endorsement. *The Christian Post.* Retrieved August 24, 2012, from http://www.christianpost.com/news/evangelical-leaders-plan-texas-meeting-to-discuss-possible-endorsement-66425/

Ward, A. (2008). *The slaves' war: The Civil War in the words of former slaves.* New York: Houghton Mifflin Harcourt.

The White House. Office of the Press Secretary. (2012, February 2). Remarks by the president at the National Prayer Breakfast. Retrieved August 24, 2012, from http://www.whitehouse.gov/the-press-office/2012/02/02/remarks-president-national-prayer-breakfast

Winseman, A. L. (2004, August 17). *Race and religion: The Protestant-Catholic divide.* Retrieved August 24, 2012, from http://www.gallup.com/poll/12718/race-religion-protestantcatholic-divide.aspx

## CHAPTER V: AGE AND RELIGION: THE FASCINATING RELATIONSHIP

Cromie, W. J. (1998, October 1). Why women live longer than men. *The Harvard University Gazette*. Retrieved August 24, 2012, from http://news.harvard.edu/gazette/1998/10.01/WhyWomenLiveLon.html

Deaton, A. S. (2009). *Aging, religion, and health* (NBER working paper no. 15271). National Bureau of Economic Research. Retrieved August 29, 2012, from http://www.nber.org/papers/w15271.pdf

Facts and statistics about the baby boomer generation. (2012, February 25). *BabyBoomer-Magazine.com*. Retrieved August 24, 2012, from http://www.babyboomer-magazine.com/news/165/ARTICLE/1437/2010-04-04.html

Funk, T. (2009, January 30). Why did I survive? Passengers struggle with why their lives were spared as jet landed in Hudson River. *The Southern Illinoisan*. Retrieved August 29, 2012, from http://thesouthern.com/lifestyles/faith-and-values/article_6417858a-8964-564c-ad63-99e5aa47fdf4.html

Gallup, G., Jr. (1991). *The Gallup Poll: Public opinion 1990*. Wilmington, DE: Scholarly Resources Inc.

Hamilton, B. E., & Sutton, P. D. (2012). *Recent trends in births and fertility rates through December 2011*. Centers for Disease Control and Prevention, National Center for Health Statistics. Retrieved August 24, 2012, from http://www.cdc.gov/nchs/data/hestat/births_fertility_december_2011/births_fertility_december_2011.htm

Mather, M., & Lavery, D. (2010, September). *In U.S., proportion married at lowest recorded levels*. Retrieved August 24, 2012, from the Population Reference Bureau website: http://www.prb.org/Articles/2010/usmarriagedecline.aspx

Quinn, S. (2010, December 16). Rethinking Elizabeth Edwards. *The Washington Post*. Retrieved August 29, 2012, from http://onfaith. washingtonpost.com/onfaith/panelists/sally_quinn/2010/12/ rethinking_elizabeth_edwards.html

## CHAPTER VI: STATE CULTURES OF RELIGION: WHY MISSISSIPPI IS VASTLY DIFFERENT FROM VERMONT

Finke, R., & Stark, R. (2005). *The churching of America, 1776-2005: Winners and losers in our religious economy.* New Brunswick, NJ: Rutgers University Press.

Grier, P. (2010, December 21). 2010 census results: Why did US population growth slow? *The Christian Science Monitor.* Retrieved August 30, 2012, from http://www.csmonitor.com/USA/Politics/ The-Vote/2010/1221/2010-census-results-Why-did-US-population-growth-slow

Jones, J. (2009, January 28). *State of the states: Political party affiliation.* Retrieved August 24, 2012, from http://www.gallup.com/ poll/114016/state-states-political-party-affiliation.aspx

McPhee, J. (1977). *Coming into the country.* New York: Farrar, Straus and Giroux.

2010 U.S. individual income tax return for Mitt and Ann Romney. Retrieved August 31, 2012, from http://www.mittromney.com/ learn/mitt/tax-return/main

U.S. Census Bureau. (n.d.). Resident population data: Population change. Retrieved August 30, 2012, from http://2010.census. gov/2010census/data/apportionment-pop-text.php

## CHAPTER VII: MEN AND WOMEN

The Baptist faith and message. (n.d.). Retrieved August 29, 2012, from the Southern Baptist Convention website: http://www.sbc.net/bfm/bfm2000.asp

Colonial life: Work, family, faith. (2012, January 8). Retrieved August 29, 2012, from the Academic American History website: http://www.academicamerican.com/colonial/topics/coloniallife.html

Davis, K., & Moore, W. E. (1945). Some principles of stratification. *American Sociological Review, 10*(2), 242-249.

*The ESV study Bible, English standard version.* (2008). Wheaton, IL: Crossway Bibles.

Gallup, G. H., Jr. (2002, December 17). *Why are women more religious?* Retrieved August 25, 2012, from http://www.gallup.com/poll/7432/why-women-more-religious.aspx

General Social Survey website (n.d.). http://www3.norc.org/GSS+Website/

Jackson, D. (2012, April 10). Obama: Tax the rich to help grow the economy. *USA Today.* Retrieved August 29, 2012, from http://content.usatoday.com/communities/theoval/post/2012/04/obama-tax-the-rich-to-grow-the-economy/1#.T8fL8fldn8c

Kanazawa, S. (2010, September 12). Why are women more religious than men? *Psychology Today.* Retrieved August 25, 2012, from http://www.psychologytoday.com/blog/the-scientific-fundamentalist/201009/why-are-women-more-religious-men-i

Lakewood Church website. (n.d.). http://www.lakewood.cc/Pages/Home.aspx

msnbc.com staff, et al. Census: Women equal to men in college degrees. (2010, April 20). *NBC News.* Retrieved August 27, 2012, from http://www.msnbc.msn.com/id/36663479/ns/us_news-census_2010/t/census-women-equal-men-college-degrees/

Occupy Wall Street website. (n.d.). http://occupywallst.org/

O'Connor, K. (2010). *Gender and women's leadership: A reference handbook.* Thousand Oaks, CA: Sage Publications, Inc.

Pomerantz, D. (2011, October 4). Entertainment's highest-earning women. *Forbes.* Retrieved August 29, 2012, from http://www.forbes.com/sites/dorothypomerantz/2011/10/04/entertainments-highest-earning-women/

Raines, J. (Ed.). (2002). *Marx on religion.* Philadelphia: Temple University Press.

Roth, M. (2011, November 14). The inequality debate: Conservatives, liberals debate what rise of rich means. *Pittsburgh Post-Gazette.* Retrieved August 29, 2012, from http://www.post-gazette.com/stories/local/region/the-inequality-debate-conservatives-liberals-debate-what-rise-of-rich-means-323838/?p=2

Stark, R. (2002). Physiology and faith: Addressing the "universal" gender difference in religious commitment. *Journal for the Scientific Study of Religion, 41*(3), 495-507.

Stephens, P., Leach, A., Taggart, L., & Jones, H. (1998). *Think sociology.* Cheltenham, U.K.: Stanley Thornes (Publishers) Ltd.

Toossi, M. (2002). A century of change: the U.S. labor force, 1950-2050. *Monthly Labor Review, 125*(5).

The United Methodist Church. (n.d.). *Mission and ministry.* Retrieved August 25, 2012, from http://www.umc.org/site/c.lwL4KnN1LtH/b.2295473/k.7034/Mission_and_Ministry.htm

Wilcox, W. B. (2007, May). As the family goes. *First Things*. Retrieved August 25, 2012, from http://www.firstthings.com/article/2007/04/as-the-family-goes-14

Wilson's war 'sociobiology.' (2012, April 2). *The Daily Beast*. Retrieved August 31, 2012, from http://www.thedailybeast.com/newsweek/2012/04/01/wilson-s-war-sociobiology.html

Wingfield, M. (2000, November 6). Can biology explain why women are more religious than men? *Baptist Standard*. Retrieved August 25, 2012, from http://www.baptiststandard.com/2000/11_6/pages/biology.html

Winseman, A. L. (2002, December 3). *Religion and gender: A congregation divided*. Retrieved August 25, 2012, from http://www.gallup.com/poll/7336/Religion-Gender-Congregation-Divided.aspx

Women and the priesthood. (2004). Retrieved August 29, 2012, from Catholic Answers website: http://www.catholic.com/tracts/women-and-the-priesthood

Wright, R. (2005, November 1). 35 who made a difference: Edward O. Wilson. Smithsonian.com. Retrieved August 31, 2012, from http://www.smithsonianmag.com/people-places/wilson.html

## CHAPTER VIII: RELIGION IS A CLASS ACT

Allan, K. (2010). *Explorations in classical sociological theory: Seeing the social world*. Thousand Oaks, CA: Pine Forge Press.

Catholic groups sue to stop birth control coverage rule. (2012, May 22). *Kaiser Health News*. Retrieved August 30, 2012, from http://www.kaiserhealthnews.org/daily-reports/2012/may/22/catholic-contraception-coverage-rule-lawsuit.aspx

Comes, L. (n.d.). Can you perceive it? Retrieved August 30, 2012, from Joel Osteen Ministries website: http://www.joelosteen.com/ HopeForToday/ThoughtsOn/Finances/CanYouPerceiveit/Pages/ CanYouPerceiveit.aspx

Conrad, J. (2007). *Fantastic reality: Marxism and the politics of religion.* London: JC Publications.

Davidson, J. D. (2008). Religious stratification: Its origins, persistence, and consequences. *Society of Religion 69*(4), 371-395.

Davidson, J. D., & Pyle, R. E. (2011). *Ranking faiths: Religious stratification in America.* Lanham, MD: Rowman & Littlefield Publishers, Inc.

*The ESV study Bible, English standard version.* (2008). Wheaton, IL: Crossway Bibles.

Falsani, C. (n.d.). The prosperity gospel. *The Washington Post.* Retrieved August 29, 2012, from http://www.washingtonpost.com/wp-srv/ special/opinions/outlook/worst-ideas/prosperity-gospel.html

Hastings, A. (Ed.). (1999). *A world history of Christianity.* London: Wm. B. Eerdmans Publishing Co.

Joel Osteen. (n.d.). Retrieved August 30, 2012, from Joel Osteen Ministries website: http://www.joelosteen.com/About/Pages/ AboutJoel.aspx

Jones, J. M. (2012, June 21). *Atheists, Muslims see most bias a presidential candidates.* Retrieved August 25, 2012, from http://www. gallup.com/poll/155285/Atheists-Muslims-Bias-Presidential-Candidates.aspx

Kim, S. H. (2012). Max Weber. *The Stanford Encyclopedia of Philosophy.* (Fall 2012 edition). Edward N. Zalta (ed.). [Forthcoming URL: http://plato.stanford.edu/archives/fall2012/entries/weber/]. Retrieved August 31, 2012, from http://plato.stanford.edu/ entries/weber/

MacArthur, J. (2006). *The MacArthur study Bible*. Nashville, TN: Thomas Nelson Inc.

Newport, F. (1979). The religious switcher in the United States. *American Sociological Review, 44*, 528-552.

Niebuhr, H. R. (2004). *The social sources of denominationalism*. Whitefish, MT: Kessinger Publishing. (Original work published 1929)

The Pew Forum on Religion & Public Life. (2008). U.S. religious landscape survey. Retrieved August 29, 2012, from http://religions.pewforum.org/pdf/report-religious-landscape-study-full.pdf

The Pew Forum on Religion & Public Life. (2009). *Faith in flux: Changes in religious affiliation in the U.S.* Retrieved August 31, 2012, from http://www.pewforum.org/uploadedfiles/Topics/Religious_Affiliation/fullreport.pdf

The Pew Forum on Religion & Public Life. (2009, January 15). The religious affiliations of U.S. presidents. Retrieved August 31, 2012, from http://www.pewforum.org/The-Religious-Affiliations-of-US-Presidents.aspx

The United Methodist Church. (2008). *Roots, 1736-1816*. Retrieved August 30, 2012, from http://www.umc.org/site/apps/nlnet/content.aspx?c=lwL4KnN1LtH&b=5399351&ct=6470771&notoc=1

Weber, M. (2002). *The Protestant ethic and the "spirit" of capitalism and other writings*. (P. Baehr & G. C. Wells, Eds., Trans.). New York: Penguin Books.

The White House. Office of the Press Secretary. (2012, February 2). Remarks by the president at the National Prayer Breakfast. Retrieved August 24, 2012, from http://www.whitehouse.gov/the-press-office/2012/02/02/remarks-president-national-prayer-breakfast

Works of Karl Marx 1843: A contribution to the critique of Hegel's philosophy of right. (n.d.). Retrieved August 31, 2012, from http://www.marxists.org/archive/marx/works/1843/critique-hpr/ intro.htm

## CHAPTER IX: THE POTENTIAL FOR A MORE DIRECT INFLUENCE OF RELIGION

Berger, P. L. (1967). *The sacred canopy: Elements of a sociological theory of religion.* New York: Anchor Books.

Broach, C. U. (1950). *Dr. Frank: An informal biography of Frank H. Leavell, leader of Baptist youth.* Nashville, TN: Broadman Press.

Causes: The Woman's Christian Temperance Union. (n.d.). Retrieved August 30, 2012, from The National Women's History Museum website: http://www.nwhm.org/online-exhibits/progressiveera/ wctu.html

The Ethics & Religious Liberty Commission website. (2012). http:// erlc.com/

Flippen, J. B. (2011). *Jimmy Carter, the politics of family, and the rise of the religious right.* Athens, GA: The University of Georgia Press.

Hughes, S. (2012, February 26). Santorum: 'I almost threw up' after reading JFK speech on church, state. *The Wall Street Journal.* Retrieved August 24, 2012, from http://blogs.wsj.com/ washwire/2012/02/26/santorum-i-almost-threw-up-after-reading-jfk-speech-on-church-state/

Surowiecki, J. (2005). *The wisdom of crowds.* New York: Random House, Inc.

Weber, M. (2002). *The Protestant ethic and the "spirit" of capitalism and other writings.* (P. Baehr & G. C. Wells, Eds., Trans.). New York: Penguin Books.

Woman's Christian Temperance Union website (n.d.). http://www.wctu.org/index.html

Young, N. J. (2012, January 19). There they go again. *The New York Times*. Retrieved August 29, 2012, from http://campaignstops.blogs.nytimes.com/2012/01/19/there-they-go-again/

# ACKNOWLEDGEMENTS

I would like to acknowledge the guidance and editing of the team at Gallup Press in the writing of this book: Geoff Brewer, Kelly Henry, Julie Ray, Trista Kunce, Samantha Allemang, Bev Passerella, and Gallup Press Associate Publisher Piotr Juszkiewicz. Geoff's input and counsel throughout the process was consistently insightful and on target. Kelly's dedicated editing and re-editing guidance made everything in the book significantly better.

This book is based largely on Gallup data gathered as part of the Gallup Healthways Well-Being Index project. Begun in January 2008, this project involves an unprecedented commitment to interviewing 1,000 Americans each night, resulting in more than 350,000 interviews a year. The fact that each interview contains core religion questions provides a unique ability to look at religion in America today in a depth heretofore not possible. Jim Clifton, Gallup Chairman and CEO, was instrumental in developing and championing the daily tracking project. Jim has, over the years, maintained a strong and unswerving dedication to Gallup's commitment to measuring and understanding public opinion.

All of Gallup's extensive focus on measuring and analyzing U.S. public opinion depends on a dedicated team of outstanding professionals. This team includes Jeff Jones, Lydia Saad, Lymari Morales, Elizabeth Mendes, Dan Witters, Sangeeta Agrawal,

Lauren Kannry, Alyssa Brown, Mark Stiemann, Lauren Wrobel, and many others.

This book is dedicated to George H. Gallup Jr. George passed away in 2011 — a great loss to all of us who knew him. George was committed all of his professional life to the scientific study of religion through survey research. His life and relationship to others also exemplified his strong personal commitment to religion. I'm proud to have been his friend.

My wife, Kim, supported me throughout the writing of this book. In fact, she pushed me to write it in the first place and kept the pressure up as I worked on its various iterations. Kim always has the big picture in mind, and I would not have been able to write it without her help and support.

# ABOUT THE AUTHOR

Frank Newport, Gallup Editor-in-Chief and one of the nation's leading public opinion analysts, has spent the major part of his working life studying public opinion — much of that opinion about religion. Newport earned a Ph.D. in sociology from the University of Michigan and has worked as a college professor, as a partner in a market research firm, and as Gallup's chief pollster for more than 20 years. He is the former president of the American Association for Public Opinion Research. The son of a Southern Baptist theologian, Newport grew up in that tradition in Texas and graduated from Baylor University. Newport's religious background and his current role as a neutral social scientist give him a unique ability to probe the reality of religion in the United States today.

Gallup Press exists to educate and inform the people who govern, manage, teach, and lead the world's 7 billion citizens. Each book meets Gallup's requirements of integrity, trust, and independence and is based on Gallup-approved science and research.